GW00787329

Hildebrand's Travel Guide
Seychelles

Publisher
K+G, KARTO+GRAFIK Verlagsgesellschaft mbH
© All rights reserved by
K+G, KARTO+GRAFIK Verlagsgesellschaft mbH
Schönberger Weg 15-17
6000 Frankfurt/Main 90
Fourth Expanded and Updated Edition 1990
Printed in Germany
ISBN 3-88989-122-5

Distributed in the United Kingdom by
Harrap Columbus,
19-23 Ludgate Hill,
London, EC4M 7PD
Tel: (01) 248 6444

Distributed in the United States by
Hunter Publishing Inc.,
300 Raritan Center Parkway,
Edison, New Jersey 08818
Tel: (201) 225 1900

Author
Clausjürgen Eicke
Contributions by:
Christine Hedegaard and Wolfgang Debelius

Photo Credits
Clausjürgen Eicke, Armgard-Dina Eicke, Dieter Lampe
Christine Henze, Jürgen W. Laupert,
Helmut Debelius/IKAN, Reinhard Scheiblich/IKAN

Illustrations
Eckart Müller, Peter Rank, Manfred Rup

Cartography
K+G, KARTO+GRAFIK Verlagsgesellschaft mbH

Translation
Bernadette Boyle, Bernd Peyer, Helmut Taylor

Lithography
PPWS, Lorenz, 6000 Frankfurt/Main 70
Haußmann-Repro, 6100 Darmstadt
Spandau-Repro, 6500 Mainz-Finthen

Type Setting
Atelier Schulz, 6050 Offenbach

Printed by
Schwab Offset KG, 6452 Hainburg/Hess.

Hildebrand's Travel Guide

Impressions

Photographs
Travel Experiences and Reflections

Information

Land and People
ABC of the Islands and Beaches
Useful Information
Contents

Supplement: Travel Map

Captions

1. Victoria's Clock Tower, the most prominent feature and characteristic landmark of the capital city. Modelled after the original standing on London's Vauxhall Bridge Road, it was erected here in 1903 when the Seychelles became a British colony.

2. Traditional palm-thatched houses such as the one shown here (just off the west coast road, near Barbarons) can still be seen today in more remote regions. Their owners appreciate the "ventilation" provided by the green canopy as well as the protection from the sun and heat.

3. European settlers and African slaves joined to form a mixed race in which every shade of skin colour is represented. Indians and other Asian immigrants have also left their mark. Not only the children, but all of the various people live here together in harmony.

4.-6. They are known as the "Seychellois" (the name they have given themselves is "Seselwa"). Some here even speak of a self-assured "new race". And, true enough, you will meet people in the Seychelles who are absolutely unique.

7.-8. The market in Victoria on a Saturday morning is usually a very gay occasion. People don't come here for the sake of produce alone – though there is an incredible variety, especially of fruit and vegetables – but also for the chance to have a little chat. The Seychellois are a communicative people and love to talk to each other in their own Creole language, the French elements of which give it a melodious sound.

9. As piped water is not available everywhere, long trips to the nearest stream are not uncommon. The Seychellois place great value on cleanliness and a smart appearance.

10. One of the most popular places to do the washing is along the St. Louis River just off Bel Air Road, a mere hundred yards from Victoria's Revolution Avenue. The laundry is slapped against the smooth surface of the rounded rocks until clean and then left in the sun to dry. A perfect occasion to exchange the latest gossip!

11. Fish constitutes the Seychellois' main source of protein and, along with rice and breadfruit, is a dietary staple. It is mostly caught in small boats averaging 5 to 10 metres (16-32 ft) in length. As can be observed here along Beau Vallon Bay, the catch brought in from coastal waters is rather modest – usually just enough to cover personal needs, with an occasional fish left over to sell.

12.   A typical way of bundling up fish for sale: strips of palm leaves are threaded through gills and mouth. In this fashion, 15 to 20 fish can easily be carried in each hand to the market. The customer, in turn, does not need a bag to take his fish home.

13.   As far as traffic is concerned, life on La Digue has not changed in ages. With just a few exceptions, automobiles are still banned here. Those who insist upon being driven, such as a tourist with luggage, will have to make do with ox-carts, an environmentally sound and highly enjoyable means of transportation. Alternative ways to navigate the narrow, palm-lined paths are on foot or by bike.

14.   It takes a somewhat larger boat (10-13 metres/32-44 ft) and "crew" to make it safely across the reef's surf.

15./16.   The magnificent and incredibly varied marine fauna will enthral skin and scuba divers alike. The different species of fish found in the waters around the Seychelles number in the hundreds. Above (15) a red snapper, below (16) two sleepers.

17.   A dream beach in the Seychelles: fine white sand washed by the glistening foam of a turquoise sea; waving palms and red granite rock cast shadows under an azure sky. It may sound like a cliché, but that's the way it really is at beaches like Anse Intendance on Mahé, Grand Anse on La Digue, Anse Lazio on Praslin and many others.

18./21.   The most famous botanical rarity of the Seychelles: the coco-de-mer. It takes 800 to 1,000 years for this palm to reach its full height of about 40 metres (130 ft). The two-lobed nut of the palm (21) matures in about seven years and can weigh up to 30 or 40 pounds. Other than a few scattered examples found on the island of Curieuse and in Mahé's botanical garden (our photograph), Praslin is the only place on earth where this palm - numbering about 4,000 - grows.

19./20.   The flora of the Seychelles is uniquely rich in species (many of them endemic) and truly magnificent in its exotic splendour. Our two examples: Blackeyed Susan (19) and tropical hanging hibiscus (20).

22.-25.   Typical for the so-called granite islands of the Seychelles: the fascinating combination of ocean and wooded heights, interspersed by grey or reddish granite rock formations. The view from different points gives an impression of the great variety offered by this wonderful landscape: Anse Takamaka/South Mahé (22); a view of Victoria's harbour from Belvedere (23); the calm waters of Anse à la Mouche (24) and the occasionally rougher bay of Port Glaud (25), both of which are located on the west coast.

26. Anse Volbert on Praslin: one of the longest, widest and most beautiful beaches of the granite isles. It slopes gently into the crystal-clear sea, all the way to the reef. At low tide, when there is no wind (as in the case of this photograph shot in May), the water is so smooth and warm that one has the impression of being in a giant natural bathtub.

27. Bird Island: one of two coral islands (the other being Denis Island) that can be reached by plane from Mahé in about 30-40 minutes. A beautiful island, lined with white coral beaches, bedecked with palms and casuarina trees, and home to a unique colony of sea birds.

28. Between April/May and October/November millions of sooty terns come to brood and rear their young on Bird Island. At times the air is full of their cries and the sky darkens when the huge flocks take flight. Their breeding grounds take up about a third of the island.

29. Competition for a nesting-place on the bare ground of the treeless part of the island leads to bitter conflicts. Victorious partners found a new family with a single egg.

30. The permanent residents of Bird Island are white terns, beautiful to behold and elegant in flight. They share the island with brown noddies, zebra doves and red fodies, as well as two giant turtles, the owner of the island and the personnel he requires to serve a maximum of 50 guests. The latter are housed in palm-thatched bungalows.

31. Sunset in the Seychelles: a dream-like experience. View from Beau Vallon Bay on Mahé with Silhouette Island on the horizon.

The Seychellois

The inhabitants of the Seychelles, the Seychellois, are a likeable people. One might even envy them a little: they enjoy a wonderful climate and the rich tropical environment, providing them with coconuts, fruit, fish and vegetable, makes it relatively easy for them to meet their basic daily requirements. And they benefit from their own light-hearted outlook on life, which is more concerned with today than tomorrow or the days after.

Again and again we perceive scenes that give us pleasure and make us smile inwardly: a Seychellois strolling home in the midday heat, a bundle of fish tied up with a palm thong in his hand, a slightly battered straw hat placed at a jaunty angle on the back of his head. "Thank God its Friday" is the message on his faded T-Shirt, but it really seems to matter very little that it is only Monday.

Certainly, the Seychellois enjoy Sundays and take advantage of every opportunity to be merry – in this sense they are no different from peoples elsewhere in the world. Their good-naturedness is especially evident in their love for music and dance. It is not always easy for them to bring this into accord with the inevitability of "daily toil". They manage, of course, to do what needs to be done in both working place and household. But, please, without any unnecessary haste or exaggeration. In this heat, who needs all the fuss? Despite all of the modern innovations, the Seychellois have managed to retain their traditional, somewhat more relaxed pace of life.

This relaxed and relatively carefree way of life even finds expression in their language, Creole, which is a kind of phonetically pleasing singsong.

To the Western visitor all of this will seem rather strange at first, but, as of the third day, it will begin to have its calming effect. Soon one will develop an ambling gait too, and one's thoughts will move at a slower pace than one is accustomed to back home.

Nature, in all its splendour, will add to the spell.

Physically, the Seychellois stand out somewhat from other islanders, such as the inhabitants of the Caribbean. Many have lighter skin colour than the Caribbean Creoles, and not a few have prominent Eurasian features. Their ancestors came primarily from Africa, India and other Asian countries, but the European influence is also evident. This is due for the greater part to French settlers who have made their home here since about the 1770's and have thus contributed markedly to the unique racial make-up of the Seychellois. It received a vital impetus with the liberation of slaves in 1835. At that time the racial ratio was thirteen African slaves to every European, a situation that was to be crucial in the development of the racial features that still predominate among the Seychellois: a relatively small and slender figure, light brown to dark skin and tightly curled hair. To speak of a "new race" may be somewhat of an exaggeration. But it is quite obvious that there are many good-looking people among the Seychellois.

Particularly the girls and young women are something to behold. Someone once described his impression of their outward and inner qualities in the following rather original terms: "French enough to have a fine figure; English enough to have proper manners; Asian enough to have a touch of the exotic; and African enough to reverberate the call of the wild". It should be added at this point that the above not only applies to the females, but to the male inhabitants of the islands as well.

An especially delightful sight are the children, dressed in their clean and proper clothes, particularly on festive occasions. (A special tip as far as picturesque sights are concerned: the Seychellois rank among the best dressed church-goers in the world. The "gala wear" you will see on such an occasion would do honour to our wedding celebrations. So, do take the trouble to get up early one Sunday morning and make your way to the nearest church!) But it is also a quaint daily sight to observe the hundreds of boys and girls in their colourful uniforms come swarming out of the school buildings during lunch hour.

On the whole, the Seychellois are a young people. Almost two thirds of the population is under 25 years of age; in 1986, for instance, there were twice as many youths between the ages of 10 and 14 as there were grown-ups between the ages of 30 and 34 years (not exactly an advanced age either).

The conspicuously large number of children also reflects another facet of the Seychellois' carefree way of life: for years now the number of legitimate children has remained under a third of the total births, and most children born out of wedlock are registered as fatherless. No wonder then, that family life in the Seychelles is primarily matriarchal, even though fathers are now increasingly concerned with the well-being of their children. This also fits in with the commonly practised division of labour: members of the older generation go out daily to their jobs in shops, hotels, administrative offices or in the ever-expanding field of agriculture. In most households it is the grandparents who remain at home to take care of children and the other members of their usually *very* extended family.

(Hedegaard)

Seychelles - Something about a Thousand Miles

When a British governor described the Seychelles' unusual geographic position as "a thousand miles out of this world", it was something of an anecdote. Yet he was not really that far from the truth, if one equates Africa with the world as it was then known. The Seychelles lie about 1,850 km (1,150 miles) to the east of Mombasa (which is almost exactly 1,000 nautical miles). One also has to credit the governor for finding a very diplomatic definition of the term "isolation", which at that time was undoubtedly understood as "exile" instead. The fact that the Seychelles remained isolated until relatively recently (to be exact, until an international flight network was established in 1971) is demonstrated by the fact that the Cypriot archbishop Makarios was sent into exile there by the British in 1956/57.

This one-time isolation has since become a profitable aspect of tourism. "Seychelles – Unique by a Thousand Miles" is now a popular slogan in tourist advertising aimed at stimulating the industry and reversing the stagnation it has experienced in recent years. And the people who created the slogan are quite right; perhaps we might even say that they are overly modest. The uniqueness they ascribe to these islands within an area of 1,000 miles holds up to comparison on a much wider scale – namely, with any other spot in this wide world. Countless large and small islands are found amidst the oceans of the world, some of coral and others of volcanic origin. But nowhere else will one find anything like the granite isles of the Seychelles! And nowhere else are there the same wide or intimately secluded beaches, so typical of the Seychelles with their mighty, rounded granite boulders. They are unmistakeably unique.

But that is not all. The Seychelles have still more things to offer that one

won't find elsewhere in the world. They have been a veritable "Noah's Ark" of nature and abound with exceptional flora and fauna, both of which have been developing undisturbed for millions of years and continue to be relatively "intact" today. One example is the fabled coco-de-mer with its bi-lobed rounded nuts; it grows exclusively in the Seychelles (primarily on the island of Praslin and to a lesser extent on the neighbouring isle of Curieuse). Once thought to grow on the bottom of the sea, it is just one of 80 species of plants endemic to the Seychelles. The animal kingdom is represented, among others, by 17 species of land birds. Scientists and hobby-ornithologists travel far to get here since these birds can't be observed in any other place on earth. Their number includes the black paradise flycatcher, which was near extinction, but has since increased in numbers again in a special reserve on the island of La Digue.

To return to the topic of the aforementioned thousand miles: this is the greatest distance within the Seychelles archipelago, which extends for about 400,000 km^2 (155,000 mi^2) over the seemingly endless expanses of the Indian Ocean. This corresponds approximately with the size of West Germany, the three Benelux countries (Belgium, Holland, Luxembourg) and Austria. Within this huge area, the total surface area of land made up by the islands of the Seychelles collectively is a mere 400 km^2 (155 mi^2), or about the size of Greater London.

Mr. Grimshaw and the Ghosts of Moyenne

In the midst of the Ste. Anne Marine National Park lies Moyenne, one of the smaller islands dotted around the main island of Mahé and themselves encircled by fine, gently sloping beaches. Full- or half-day boat trips can be arranged from Victoria; it takes about 20 minutes to reach Moyenne. Upon mooring in the warm and shallow waters along the shoreline, one is greeted by the owner of the island, Brendon Grimshaw. If one is to lend credence to his stories, there is a pirate's treasure still hidden somewhere on the island. Two-hundred-year-old historical documents mention two graves on the island which supposedly contain a treasure. Up until now, however, no one really knows if this is actually true. But the topic continues to occupy the thoughts of the island's present owner. He even claims that speculations regarding the treasure have surfaced again just recently. In 1974 a girl in Mahé dreamed of a mango tree growing next to the graves, under which the treasure was to be found. She had never been to Moyenne previously. Although her dream was not given much credence at the time, heavy rainfall some time later washed away the soil and revealed yet another grave on the exact spot the girl had seen in her dream.

While showing us around the island, Grimshaw tell us his strange tale of how he was almost killed by two falling coconuts just seconds after he first broke the ground there with a spade. He immediately ceased digging.

Equally mysterious, he confides in us, is the fact that a divining rod will dip at that same spot as well as in some other location where he presumes another treasure to be.

Grimshaw tells a number of other amusing ghost stories, embellishing them with personal experiences of rattling windowpanes and banging doors, all of which help to induce chills among his listeners.

The shady path that skirts the island also leads past two ruins. One of them, known as the "Dog House", was originally built as an asylum for dogs by a British lady. She lived on the island between 1899 and 1914, taking care of stray dogs she picked up in neighbouring Mahé.

The path comes to an end at an old Creole villa, which has been restored and now offers tourists a shady veranda for a moment of respite. A cool beer or fresh coconut drink work wonders now!

A few paces from here one has a magnificent view of Mahé's mountains and the turquoise waters of the Marine National Park.

(Hedegaard)

Highlights

The words **"Bus Stop"** have been stencilled on the simple sign marking the point where the bus to south Mahé departs. The red letters on their white background – similar to those used on wooden packing cases – must have struck those responsible for the sign as a little austere ... simply not colourful enough. Alternatively, thought might have been given to those who – in the jargon of sign writers – need a "visual signal". In any case, a bright green bus complete with black and white tyres has been added to the sign. Most naive in its execution, the picture adds a cheery touch to the side of the road. Riding on a bus becomes a pleasure even before our journey begins.

The old trucks which used to ferry people about on hard wooden benches have long since ended up in scrap yards. Nowadays, small grey-green buses provide a service which is as regular as transport needs – and the mood of the driver – dictate. Tourists, of course, are usually seen zipping around in airy "Mini Mokes" or taxis. Which would explain why the presence of one of their breed in a bus will often be greeted by an unmistakable, if short-lived, stir of surprise. Soon enough, however, passengers local and foreign will return to the matter at hand – which, when you're on a bus in the Seychelles, means chatting with your neighbour.

You could easily think you were in a different world: gone are all notions of keeping to yourself while involved in the serious business of getting from A

Bus Stop

to B. Instead, prepare for an atmosphere which is casual, carefree and very communicative! The motley crew of gaily-dressed passengers prove to be willing and vivacious conversationalists. There are elderly women in wide-brimmed raffia hats cradling bags of vegetables in their laps. A young mother is out with her two delightful little girls: the eldest has been entrusted with their fare and politely hands this to the conductor. Both girls have braided hair tied with bright ribbons – not shiny silk but strips of colourful fabric cut, no doubt, from articles of clothing which have been outgrown. Diagonally opposite, there's an old man – or does he only seem so old because his hands have been toughened by manual work and his face lined and weathered by the sun? He, too, has a shady hat ... unlike the young people nearby, who sport jeans, open-necked shirts and those much sought-after quartz watches. They represent the new generation of Seychellois. One of the young men is carrying a smart briefcase (you inevitably find yourself wondering where he could be headed, what he might be carrying?); another is enjoying an animated conversation with the driver, whose attention is thus surely dis-

tracted from the unforeseen hazards which could well lurk ahead on these narrow roads. Slightly alarming, but then the Seychellois are – thank goodness – naturals at the wheel. Theirs is not recklessness or bravado but the kind of ease which seems at times almost to verge upon the languid. It is this very particular easy-going pace which characterizes life in the Seychelles.

My neighbour turns to me with the standard questions put to tourists: what's my name, where do I come from, how do I like the Seychelles? Then, without making any further inquiries, he begins to talk about himself quite openly. He tells me that he has recently found a job as a truck-driver – and that after a long period of unemployment. He's very happy at this work but the money doesn't go very far with prices as high as they are. Remarking that he hopes to marry soon, he shows me a picture of his girlfriend and goes on to explain that she works in a shop in Victoria and that between the two of them they should be able to manage. I immediately warm to the candid, unaffected manner of my companion – it is a feeling I experience again and again in the course of my stay and must surely be one of the most lasting impressions of the islands. Part of their magic is the way people treat each other in a friendly, unconstrained manner, are genuinely interested in the other person, and are free from aggression. The bus proves to be a good place to observe just that.

In the **Vallée de Mai** on Praslin it would be easy to imagine one had been transported back to prehistoric times. Only the carefully laid-out paths (equally painstakingly maintained by hard-working Seychellois women with their almost obligatory sunhats) remind one that human hands have been (and still are) at work here, opening the homeland of the coco-de-mer to visitors.

Just a few yards from the parking lot and we are in the thick of a verdant palm grove; shafts of sunlight pierce the foliage above and shed shimmering lights onto the vegetation below. The leaves of young coco-de-mer palms – no more than saplings in fact – grow directly out of the ground, spreading to form gigantic fans of several metres in width. Hardly surprising that they are a popular building and weaving material: the Seychellois use them for thatching and weave them into decorative room dividers (*macoutis*), mats, baskets and airy sun hats. The leaves of older palms – those which have developed a trunk – stretch towards the heavens at the end of long stems ... only to be dragged down towards the ground again by their own weight. Mature palms, some 20-30 metres (65-100 ft) in height, sway in the breeze like metronomes. Under the ample weight of their multiple fruits, their movements are slow and deliberate. Coco-de-mer palms usually bear three to five of the double coconuts but in some cases there can be as many as ten, of varying sizes, adding up to an impressive weight of one or even two hundred kilos. When one of these full-sized nuts fall to the ground, the dull thud it makes upon hitting the carpet of decaying leaves beneath can cause quite a stir among bystanders. But, there's no need to worry about being hit by such a ten or twenty-kilo "bombshell" as you stroll innocently along the paths: potential dangers are removed in good time.

Male palms have to be searched out – except, that is, for the one which stands (as an exhibition piece, as it were) right at the entrance to the park. The long, catkin-like male inflorescence grows out of the axils of the sturdy leaf stalks approximately half way up the palm and droops down under its own weight. Green geckos are often to be seen climbing among the many orange flowers of the pendulous inflorescence. A testimony to the ingenuity of nature, the geckos act as "pollination agents" between male and female palms.

But the coco-de-mer does not stand alone: a number of "strangers" have also become established in the Vallée de Mai. There are, for example, vacoas (also known as screw pines), of which the vacoa maroon is a particularly noteworthy specimen. The stem of this screw pine can in some instances be so stunted as to hardly exist at all; the crown of the tree is then supported by a cone-shaped arrangement of stilt-like aerial roots, which can grow to 10 m (33 ft) in length. In other places, slender palmiste palms stretch skywards, reaching impressive heights of 30 m (98 ft) and more; from the heart of the palmiste palm comes the essential ingredient of the highly prized "millionaire's salad". And then there are the normal coconut palms, though these are really only found as solitary individuals.

All together the palms form a dense canopy of leaves. If there is no wind to stir the leaves of the palms, an eerie stillness reigns beneath the canopy. A breeze, however, will soon put an end to any sense of reverie, for then the long, outstretched leaves of the coco-de-mer beat against each other with an almost metallic ring, as if two corrugated iron sheets were crashing together. The sudden din drowns out the occasional calls of the birds in the forest. It could also mean that a sound which would be music to the ears of ornithologists remains unheard: that of remnants of food dropping as a black parrot feeds in the trees above. Transfixed by the unmistakeable sound, all eyes scan the dense canopy in search of the parrot (which is in fact not so much black as dark grey to brown). If you are lucky enough to catch a glimpse of either female or male – these gregarious birds like to live in small groups – you will be looking at one of the rarest birds in the world ... and will be the envy of many a Seychellois who has waited years for such a sighting – usually to no avail.

Seychelles sunsets surely cannot be that much different from sunsets in other parts of the Tropics ... well, so we might think. And true enough, if the fiery glow of the sky after the sun has dipped beneath the horizon is our only criterion, we could even be right. But there is more to a sunset than that: other "ingredients" make all the difference ... and it these additional elements which are to be found in such astonishing variety in the Seychelles.

There are, for example, the islands. In the first instance we might mention

Silhouette: could it be that its name stems from the fact that, seen from Beau Vallon Bay, the contours of the island stand out against the glowing sky like the most accurate of cameos? Then there are the romantic islands of Cousin and Cousine. Viewed from Grand Anse on Praslin, the sight of the two isles – at times "garnished" with huge banks of billowing cloud – is truly unforgettable. Then there's La Digue, with its already pink-tinged granite cliffs that will start to glow like the dying embers of a fire in the soft evening sunlight. And on Mahé: yours the sweet sensation of contentment as, in the view from La Misère, the gold-red heavens darken, the harbour lights come on and Victoria prepares to greet the falling night.

Perhaps the most memorable experience will be sunset over Bird Island. The sun will hardly have dipped below the horizon before, suddenly, thousands upon thousands of the island's sea birds will have taken to the air to scour the ocean for food. Their shrill, haunting cries fill the air as they perform the most amazing manoeuvres in flight, plummeting vertically down into the waters then rising into the skies again whilst the ocean's waves, breaking incessantly on the even, white sandy beach, beat out a rhythmic accompaniment. Dotted with soft white clouds now highlighted by the sun's last rays, the spreading red fire of the evening sky is darkened more and more by the multitude of soaring birds. One thinks fleetingly of Hitchcock's thriller, "The Birds", but the awe-inspiring majesty of this, nature's spectacle, brooks no comparison. And, as the mantle of darkness gently clothes the shimmering white sands, should reflection pay emotion's reverie court, be it in acknowledgement of nature's grace in having allowed this marvel to unfold before one.

"Island Hopping" in the Seychelles is unique. For, whether you're a seasoned traveller – one for whom boarding an intercontinental jet is about as exciting as stepping into an elevator – or a relative beginner in the ranks of jet-age holidaymakers, hopping from island to island is sure to be both novel and exhilarating.

If you happen to be on one of the Air Seychelles' older and smaller aircraft, then with luck you might find yourself seated next to none other than the pilot. The opportunity to watch his every move, to marvel at the many instruments and dials, all of which must fulfil some very important function or they wouldn't be there, would they? And then there's the relaxed and friendly atmosphere aboard the aircraft, a result of the motley crowd on board. For island hopping is not restricted to camera-toting tourists: no, many local people, too, choose this method of moving between the islands. There'll be mothers returning home with their children, perhaps after a visit to a doctor in Victoria; grandmothers on their way to visit grandchildren; businessmen carrying important-looking briefcases; mechanics setting out to solve some technical difficulty somewhere.

All the passengers now seated in the not exactly spacious cabin had to go through a most remarkable procedure prior to takeoff from the airport

in Mahé: each one, as well as all baggage, had to be weighed! The point being that every spare kilo of payload can be used to carry necessary goods: parcels, newspapers, magazines, spare parts, etc. on the outward journey; parcels, fruit, birds' eggs and the like on the return trip.

Even the flight announcement just before takeoff was tinged with originality. The pilot turned briefly to greet his passengers with the words: "Morning. Air Seychelles. Praslin. No smoking please (points to sign). Safety instructions (holds the card up high). O.K.? Let's go." And we did.

Most passengers glance out the window from time to time. At a cruising altitude of just a few hundred metres there's always plenty to see and enjoy. Fishing boats glide across the turquoise sea, leaving the finest of foam trails to fleetingly mark their passage. Islands float on the same waters, circles of lush green tropical vegetation surrounded by a fringe of almost unbroken white sand ... and, yes, you really can make out the palm trees. Some of the islands are embellished by a further silvery ring as the tide breaks on coral reefs. Banking the aircraft slightly so as to facilitate vision, the pilot points out a school of dolphins playing in the sea below, clearing the water effortlessly, disappearing from view swiftly and gracefully. Banks of clouds stand motionless against the horizon, contrasting sharply with the bluer than blue of the sky.

As we begin our approach, the plane descends through a few clouds shuddering just slightly. Finally, just before landing, the narrow coastal strip of pale sands, palm trees and small houses looms ever closer and clearer. Touchdown on the runway that cuts straight as a die through the verdant surroundings. Engines are cut, doors opened. "Welcome!" Island hopping is wonderful.

P.S. Even if you fly with one of the larger "Twin Otter" aircraft, you'll still find island hopping an unforgettable experience. In service since 1987, these more modern planes were introduced by Air Seychelles to augment interisland air traffic.

One more thing: when the Seychellois talk about island hopping, they mean not only airborne jumps but also island travel by boat, schooner or ferry.

The market quarter of Victoria is a place where you never cease to look around, never cease to enjoy delightful discoveries. It's impossible to move at anything but a leisurely pace, yet your mind will reel under the influence of so many colourful impressions and recollections. The market scene over by the fruit stand, couldn't it be taken straight from Cabbage Row in Gershwin's *Porgy and Bess*? And that old colonial house with the wrought-iron balcony, couldn't that be a little piece of New Orleans? And then there's the alleyway with its hotchpotch of corrugated-iron huts, all standing at odd angles, all rather askew. Bright turquoises combined so boldly with rasperry-reds and brilliant yellows are surely only to be found in the Caribbean ... yet nearby we also come across merchants' stores belonging to the likes of Messrs.

Leong Thiong and S.R.K. Naiken. Their remarkable collections of goods could grace the pages of any age-old picture book: wares piled high reminiscent of Singapore's former Chinatown, a potpourri of fragrances worthy of any genuine Indian bazaar. Then there's the British connection: according to the sign at the entrance, we are entering the "Sir Selwyn Selwyn-Clarke Market"!.

All this, and then the people: here, too, they represent African, Indian, Asian and European influences on the islands, thus reflecting the past – and the present – of the Seychelles.

The hustle and bustle of trading: men carrying three or four bundles of fish in each hand head for their particular spot on the market; at the heart of the market, in the shade of the giant mango tree, women amble from stall to stall carefully comparing the prices of oranges and greens, aubergines and cassavas; children enjoy their own form of tropical "sweet" – sugar cane kindly cut for them by some stallholder and providing them with a long-lasting lollipop; mothers pause in the narrow arcade designated to butchers and contemplate a modest Sunday roast for their large families; men pass the time of day with the tobacco dealer, who weighs out a few rupees worth of the weed as their weekend ration. Standing a while to deliberate, chatting here, exchanging a friendly word with an old acquaintance there. What was that about the triplets born in Mont Fleuri? And old George is back on his feet again after all... incredible!

You just can't tear yourself away from such scenes of folklore in action. Which isn't to say that they are in any way "staged" for tourists. No, this is simply life as it is in the Seychelles! A way of life rarely found in other parts of the world today and, who knows, one which might disappear altogether in the not too distant future.

A guest of the birds... there's no mistaking the message conveyed by the sign near the landing stage of Cousin Island. The assistant warden John L. Souyana is quick to emphasize that the message is not only directed at tourists but also applies to the five people who live on the island on a more permanent basis: the scientific team under warden Roby Bresson, keepers of this paradise regained.

Disembarking from the rubber dinghy, a few steps along the soft sands of the wide beach suffice to drive that message home: nature is not subject to man here, but just the oppo-site. In 1968 Cousin Island was purchased by the International Council for Bird Preservation and declared a nature reserve. Since then the authorities have brooked no human interference in the unique flora and fauna of the island... save, that is, to ensure that potential dangers (such as predatory barn owls, cats and rats) are kept at bay. Having become established on other islands, such animals have decimated bird colonies there.

The absence of natural enemies accounts for the very unusual behaviour of the birds in the presence of man. Quite simply, they feel no fear. John has to ask explicitly that visitors draw nearer as he points out a white-tailed tropic bird which is brooding in a cavity in a tree. No flurry: the bird looks at her admirers with as much curiosity as they show for her. As a matter of course, John restores fairy tern chicks – fluffy bundles of light brown down – to the fork of a tree, whence they were blown in a storm the night before. The

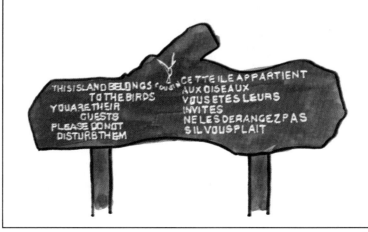

chicks usually stay in their open-air nursery for months, never moving from the spot. Even for the eggs, such a cavity provides sanctuary enough: fairy terns are satisfied with the slightest of hollows when laying their eggs.

The more time one spends wandering around the island, the greater will be one's amazement and emotion. It in fact takes about two hours to complete the circuit, allowing visitors to drink in the unspoiled nature of the environment, to stroll along the coast under giant casuarinas, to pick their way through dense palm groves and deciduous woods. An unimaginable number of birds, an unbelievable variety of species.

Looking out from a rocky outcrop to see brilliant white tropic birds and fairy terns against the turquoise of the sea; black and brown noddies brooding in the green of casuarinas and palms; frigate birds with their enormous wingspan of up to 2 m (over 6 ft) gliding as silhouettes across the bluest of skies.

Unforgettable pictures... and just as unlikely to slip from one's memory is the cacophony of sounds one hears: the screeching, skrieking and cooing of those countless birds filling the air.

Someone once aptly said that this place inspired him to devoutness. Which says it all. Unless, that is, we are so ungrateful as to be left unmoved by the small and inconspicuous brush warbler. Found nowhere else in the world, this little bird is Cousin's true ornithological sensation ... for experts far more important than the 250,000 sea birds which make the island their home.

Victoria, World's Smallest Capital

There are many capital cities where visitors inevitably feel they are under a certain obligation to keep on the move – whether it be running a sort of cultural gauntlet or being caught up in a maelstrom of entertainment and shopping. What a pleasure to find that there's none of that in Victoria!

The tiny capital (a mere 25,000 inhabitants would seem to justify the diminutive) is simply enchanting. It's easy to find one's bearings here and then to delight in a way of life which is far removed from the (probably) rather more hectic pace of home. The experience is leisurely and colourful, novel and more than charming. Which is not to say that the Seychellois from more rural areas are not impressed by the sheer pace of their capital. And, indeed, the rhythm of day-to-day life here is a deal faster than elsewhere on the islands. This is particularly true of the market, where fish and meat, fruit and vegetables, spices and gossip change hands in a friendly, informal atmosphere. The produce on offer at the market varies according to the season; it's fascinating to watch as the Seychellois develop a sharp business sense when it comes to haggling over the price of a tasty bit of fish or of a delicious papaya. In low, colourfully painted houses surrounding the market, Chinese and Indian traders display a wide range of (primarily cotton) fabrics. Vivid designs are a particular favourite among the locals. Foreign visitors are usually enthralled by the array of cotton prints and inevitably reach for their cameras in order to capture the picturesque scene on film; most, however, stop short of buying.

The serious business of shopping for pleasure is best undertaken at the heart of Victoria, in the quarter around the wrought-iron clock tower (see photo 1). Painted silver and featuring quite intricate decorative work, the clock tower has become a landmark of the capital. Some say it was modelled upon Big Ben in London, others that it's a replica of the Victoria Clock on Vauxhall Bridge Road, again in the English capital. Be that as it may, the streets around the clock tower overflow with a multitude of brightly coloured wares. Such is the case, for example, in Victoria House on the corner of Francis Rachel Street and State House Avenue, or in the boutiques along Independence Avenue. Anyone who still hasn't bought their *pareo* will find these multi-purpose lengths of cotton fabric in all possible colours and patterns. Beachwear can also be purchased here at very reasonable prices.

At the clock tower – where Independence Avenue, Victoria's most popular "shopping and *flânerie* mile", begins – souvenir stalls abound with items which are chic, others which are cheerily decorative ... and others which are just plain kitsch. Sea shells, little dolls and wickerwork, coco-demer nuts fashioned as salad bowls or reproduced in miniature, both polished to a burnished brown.

The cafe of Victoria's famous Pirates Arms Hotel is a good place to relax over a cool drink or steaming espresso and watch the world stroll by. People come here to see and be seen, to meet up with friends, to fall into easy conversation with people at neighbouring tables, to conclude a speedy business transaction.

A short distance away, an example of modern architecture provides a sharp contrast. A great, grey boxlike affair with an immense reflective glass front, the building as cold and anonymous as the arbiters of financial destiny who are at work within its confines. "Light-footed" Independence House stands nearby. The candid architecture of the yellow building seems somehow to imply that this is the headquarters of Seychelles tourism (the full title of the governing body is the Tourism Division of the Ministry of Tourism and Transport). On the ground floor of the same building you'll find the Tourist Information Office, containing all the information the average tourist could possibly need. Independence House was built just a few years ago, as was the monument on Freedom Square in front of it. The monument represents the three continents of Africa, Asia and Europe, whence the forebears of today's Seychellois migrated to the islands. A modern counterpoint to the nostalgia of the clock tower at the other end of the avenue.

(A further example of modern art can, by the way, be found on the right-hand side of 5th June Avenue. The bronze statue represents a man stretching his arms heavenwards, the chains which once bound him now shattered: it symbolizes the liberation of the Seychelles from colonialism.)

On the way back towards the clock tower, a visit to the National Museum is definitely to be recommended. Its extensive collection pertaining to the history of the Seychelles includes documents, maps, historical photographs, coins, model ships and canons, as well as the so-called Stone of Possession, erected on Mahé by the French in 1756. The natural history section of the museum features a sizeable collection of shells, corals, butterflies and coco-de-mer nuts.

When it comes time to return to your hotel, you'll usually find taxis waiting opposite the museum. If this is not the case, turn right at the clock tower and make your way to the main taxi rank (opposite St. Paul's Cathedral). Should you prefer to travel by bus, continue along Albert Street and at the end turn right into Palm Street. Here, opposite Unity House, you'll find the main bus station; buses depart to destinations all over the island, including the major hotels.

While in the vicinity of the Roman Catholic cathedral of St. Paul, pay attention to the way which the hour is struck. Providing its ancient workings are not defect, the clock strikes once on the hour proper and once again two minutes later. Someone once suggested that this was to allow the unhurried and easy-going Seychellois a second chance to get the time right.

Michael Adams, Artist

"To Mr. Adams', please." Without more ado the taxi driver puts the car in gear and sets off along the road. No questions asked as to the location or adress – he simply takes you there. Obviously, then, the man is well-known, at least among taxi drivers. This means that a lot of people must go to see him, which in turn further attests his fame.

And it proves to be just so. A conversation with Michael Adams is bound to be interrupted – unless one has made an appointment at some later hour of the day (before he retires to his 13" x 13" "jungle studio" a few paces from his house to paint while listening to classical Baroque music).

More than anyone before him, Michael Adams has tried to capture the Seychelles artistically. He has done this in such a unique and successful manner that he has become a sort of "trademark" of the Seychelles. And this despite the fact that he has only been here since 1972, after having spent years studying in England and working in East Africa. Numerous exhibitions and vernissages have made his work – and the Seychelles – known throughout the world. He would like to accomplish even more, but admits that this would be a question of time and financial means. He much prefers having people visit him. And they do: his customers include famous actors and motor-racing drivers as well as prominent figures in business and politics.

Though he is extremely lively, Michael Adams gives the impression of being a settled man. He describes himself as a "man from the woods and the jungle". Evidently, experiences and impressions gathered during his youth have played a major role. Born in 1937 as the son of a rubber tree planter in Malaya, he spent his early years, he says, within sight of the jungle. No wonder, then, that his paintings primarily depict the forest, or the jungle surrounding his home. He has, in fact, created a sort of "model" jungle directly in front of the windows of his Seychellois-style house.

Greens and yellows, together with his inimitable stroke of the brush, give his paintings a certain levity which he counterpoises by applying earthy browns – to him an essential aspect of the jungle. He mentions the "six dimensions" of his paintings, meaning that all of the senses should be stimulated by them, that viewers should be able to smell and hear the jungle as well.

Recently he has begun to include people in his paintings, obviously Seychellois, making a compositional trajectory between their rural or urban environments and nature. Sometimes he will sit in his car across from a bus stop, observing the motions of those waiting and busily setting them down on paper for future inspiration for his paintings.

A German newspaper once called him the "Gauguin of the Seychelles", a label that rather amuses him. His paintings and their style, as well as he himself and his family, are proof of the contrary. No one in the family considers they are living in isolation or "alternatively": they are simply living their own lives.

Should you wish to visit without the assistance of a friendly taxi driver, Michael Adams' studio is located near Mahé's southwestern coast, in Anse aux Poules, between Anse à la Mouche and Baie Lazare, right in the middle of the woods. A sign at the roadside states: "Michael Adams Paintings of Seychelles". Of course, one can purchase an "Adams" here – the great selection of originals or hand-signed prints in a variety of motifs and formats will not exactly facilitate your choice!
(P.S.: Michael Adams is the best known painter of the Seychelles, but not the only one. For more details of arts and crafts, galleries and workshops, see the chapter "Souvenirs".)

A Paradise for Scuba Divers and Snorkellers

A glance at the map awakes expectations: the Seychelles are almost in the middle of the Indian Ocean, far away from the huge continents and their polluted shores. But I have seen many islands with equally promising locations, whether in the Indian or the Pacific Ocean, and experience has made me sceptical whenever I hear euphoric talk of dream beaches. All the places in the tropics I have dived in so far have proven to be very similar, so that memories of specific diving sites often become difficult to recall. Would the Seychelles turn out to be different?

The Boeing rolls slightly as it makes its descent through minor turbulence. The sky is completely overcast; the islands below are a foreboding sight. Almost black, they lie there in a leaden sea, their peaks shrouded in rain clouds. But the landing is smooth and the instructor from the diving station at La Digue is already there waiting for us. He claps me heartily on the shoulder and tries to console me. After all, it never rains for more than 14 days here! I give him a rather sorry grin, for that is exactly how long I plan to stay. He herds us into something that resembles a bus and off we go towards the harbour, past Seychellois under umbrellas and incredibly lush vegetation. To the left, smooth cliffs tower into the clouds; to the right, the swells of the Indian Ocean. We get off at the harbour for the final leg of our journey: a four-hour boat ride from Mahé to La Digue. The islands appear to be close enough to touch... A huge tanker that has been anchored prompts me to speculate: "Wouldn't it make a fine wreck?!" Suddenly its rusty-red hull seems to glow. Hey folks, the sun is shining! Even the instructor breathes a sigh of relief. The setting sun produces an explosion of colours, crowned by three separate rainbows.

A dinghy makes its way towards us. Our "tub" has too much draught to take us all the way to the beach. One last waltz with the waves, a mighty jump and we've made it. A beer, a bungalow, a bed. Outside, the noises

of the jungle. We awake in the morning to the sound of gushing rain. Nothing gushing from the shower. A breakfast of ham'n'eggs, an ox-drawn cart is loaded up with tanks and off we go to the harbour where the "La Feline", our floating dive station, awaits us. We sail around the island and my astonishment begins to grow. Those huge granite boulders and the palms, a pretty sight indeed. Now that the sun is shining, everything is alright again. The anchor slides overboard and immediately there's a lot of hustling and bustling. We squeeze into our suits,

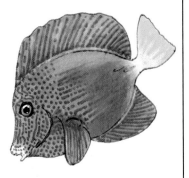

Surgeonfish

53

reach for weight belts, scream for tanks and bug our buddies with special requests. Splash... water as clear as gin and here, too, we are surrounded by mighty granite rocks. The group soon "dissolves" and I have time for a closer look at things. Much is different from, let us say, the Maldive Islands. The profuse coral growth commonly encountered in atolls is missing here altogether; apparently it didn't manage to establish itself on the primary rock of the Seychelles. But the necessary shelters for fish exist anyway, in the form of nooks, cracks, caves and overhangs. And with these shelters come all of the able swimmers such as groupers, stingrays, nurse sharks, marine turtles and cuttlefish, as well as the more cautious shrimps, crabs and lobsters. I know the different species of fish quite well and quickly notice the African influence: here, a tiny dwarf angelfish; there, a wrasse – coloured in a manner one commonly finds in Kenya. Underwater visibility is good, always about 20 metres (66 feet), there is little current and the water is warm. In other words, perfect diving conditions, especially for photographers.

Watch out for sea urchins. Unfortunately, they are all over the place, even in the daytime. A couple of the divers have already had some painful encounters. Digging the spines out of various parts of the body certainly hurts. Hardly bearable without triple cognacs. But there are few other hazards to watch out for, as larger sharks rarely venture into the area of the Seychelles Plateau, upon which all the islands are located. Here, the water reaches a maximum depth of just 70 metres (230 feet). We seldom dived

further than 25 metres (82 feet) for the simple reason that it just didn't get any deeper.

Snorkelling

Even fanatical divers like to snorkel when conditions are good. And they certainly are just that – and not only around Mahé's northern and northwestern shores or at the Ste. Anne Marine National Park. The diving sites around Praslin and La Digue also have shallow areas, for example off the islands of Saint Pierre and the Sisters, where there is much to be seen. Visibility in these shallow waters is incredible, enabling us to marvel at profuse coral formations which only grow in the protected coastal waters.

We are floating on the surface, enjoying a visibility of some 50 metres (almost 165 feet)! A quick, shallow dive and right away the small clownfish come dashing towards our masks in defence of their territory. Their "partners", the sea anemones, wear violet robes and have bright yellow tentacles. Even at a depth of 2 metres (6 $1/2$ feet), the reflection of the midday sun on the white sand is dazzling. But it gets better still: a huge school of surgeonfish suddenly materializes. Their blue bodies form a swirling mass, darting in and out of coral branches in search of algae to feed on. They hardly take notice of us snorkellers. We are fascinated. Brightly coloured parrotfish accompany us back to the waiting boat.

A diving Excursion to the "Ennerdale"

One of the highlights of a Seychelles tour is a dive down to the "Ennerdale", a huge tanker that sank off the coast of Mahé in 1969. It ran aground to the northeast of Mahé, ripping open its hull and sinking within a few hours. The accident did not lead to oil pollution because the tanker had previously been pumped dry. The British Navy afterwards dynamited the ship; fore and aft sections of the vessel were thereby separated. The main part of the hull now lies at a depth of 8-35 metres (26-115 feet) and will gladden the heart of any wreck-diving fan. Large schools of mackerel steadily patrol the upper deck while groups of batfish occupy the interior of the wreck, as if they were holding a wake, and stare bleary-eyed at their unexpected visitors. Morays house in the dynamited tanks and sponges and corals in all colours grow along gangways, valves and pipelines. One of the divers poses on a shiny toilet bowl in a crew-member's cabin; another makes believe he is steering the ship on the split-off bridge. The true guardian of the wreck is a tremendous grouper of proportions that divers usually only dream about. The multitude of fish found all around the wreck is impressive. We'll be back despite the time-consuming boat ride to and from La Digue.

On the island itself, one should not miss Grand Anse. A fairytale bay: incredibly white, powdery sand bordered by polished granite boulders and a palm forest. Having oneself transported there and back again in an ox-cart is relaxation at its very best.

Those interested in snorkelling and diving will find more information in "Fascinating Underwater World" (p.98) and "Sports in the Seychelles" (p.141).

(Debelius)

Coco-de-Mer, Fruit from the Sea

The widely travelled Portuguese seafarers were quite astonished at what they found among the "wild" inhabitants. What was this oddly shaped and unusually large fruit? And where might it have come from?

The fact that it just appeared on the beach one morning, washed in from somewhere, only offered at best a very superficial explanation and did little to clarify the mystery. Wherever such a fruit drifted ashore – whether along India's east coast, in Ceylon, the Maldives or even Indonesia – people pondered over its possible origins. One of the legends surrounding it, namely that which attributed its origin to a large underwater tree, accounts for the name given to this bi-lobed nut: coco-de-mer, "sea coconut".

The association between the doubly-rounded form and human femininity led to the belief that the coco-de-mer – especially the hard, ivory-like kernel of the ripe fruit – had some very special properties, particularly as an aphrodisiac and as a cure for all maladies resulting from advanced age. As a result

55

of this, and the fact that it was scarce, it became a highly-prized rarity. Even European rulers fell under its spell. History reports that the Hapsburg Rudolf II, emperor of the Holy Roman Empire, purchased such a nut in Prague just prior to his death in 1612; he paid the princely sum of 4,000 gold ducats, or what was then the equivalent of 500 dairy cows. His court jeweller, Anton Schweinberger, fashioned it into a richly ornamented, gold-embellished drinking vessel, which can still be seen today at the Kunsthistorisches Museum in Vienna. Further relics are found in London's British Museum; at the University of Uppsala, Sweden; in the "Grüne Gewölbe" in Dresden; and in the Provincial Overijssels Museum in Zwolle, Netherlands. Other uses for the nut have also been recorded. In China, for instance, amulets were made from the coco-de-mer. The fishermen of the Seychelles and Mauritius used the halved and hollowed out shell of the nut to bail out their boats. And, according to one eye witness, the same even served as a begging bowl in Calcutta.

The first European to see the coco-de-mer in its natural environment was the French captain Lazare Picault. During his second expedition from Mauritius to the Seychelles in 1744 he visited what is now known as the island of Praslin. Because of the numerous palms he found there, he named it l'Isle de Palme. His travel journal implies that he did see the tree, but not its fruit. Thus the coco-de-mer remained shrouded in mystery for another 24 years, until the arrival of the surveyor Barré in 1768, a member of the expedition led by the Chevalier

Dufresne. He must be credited as the true – in botanical terms – discoverer of both tree and its fruit.

The aura enjoyed by the coco-de-mer as the "fruit that came from the sea" and as an exotic rarity promptly vanished. The island of Praslin now had to supply whole shiploads of the much sought-after nuts. As always happens when there is insufficient

knowledge of the laws of supply and demand, the sudden surfeit had devastating effects: the market for the nuts collapsed from one day to the next. Not only the disappointed traders felt the consequences, but also Nature itself. A mere 4,000 coco-de-mer palms remained, limited to a relatively small and isolated area at the centre of Praslin. Today, this area, the Vallée de Mai National Park, is strictly protected. Other than a few palms on the neighbouring island of Curieuse, this is the only place in the world where the coco-de-mere grows, and it will probably remain the only one in the future. For a number of reasons.

In the first place, the processes of reproduction and growth of the double nut are extremely slow. When the ripe fruit falls to the ground, nothing at all happens for about six months – it simply rests. Germination and root-taking require three years and another seven years go by before the seedling matures. It will take twenty-five years until it begins to bear fruit and no less than a thousand years to reach its full size! The larger specimens found in Vallée de Mai – about 40 metres (130 feet) in height – are estimated to be 800 years old.

Secondly, the sheer size and weight of the fruit (the heaviest in the world, it has been known to weigh up to 40 pounds) further hinder its natural distribution. The nut, when capable of germination, sinks in water like a piece of lead, and thus can't be carried by currents. But that's not all: salt water will soon destroy the seedling.

This, by the way, also explains how the coco-de-mer nut did reach distant shores after all. When the seedling dies it decomposes very quickly; the nut becomes lighter and then becomes buoyant.

There is yet another factor that makes the propagation of these palms problematic (even when planted by hand): the female palm, which carries the precious fruit, needs to have a male tree in its immediate vicinity. The latter has an olive green catkin about 5-6 centimetres thick and close to a metre long, which has as much similarity with parts of the human anatomy as the female coco-de-mer does. This likeness has, of course, further inspired the imagination of the Seychellois. They believe that the loud sound produced as the long palm leaves (up to 6 metres/20 feet in length) slap against each other on stormy nights is the sound made when the male and female palms unite. Of course, no one has ever seen this with their own eyes; to do so, continues the legend, would inevitably bring about terrible consequences. Reality, however, is somewhat less colourful. The union between the orange-coloured blossoms of the stamen and the female palms is consummated by way of insects, the green gecko or the wind.

Under the control of the government, three thousand coco-de-mer nuts are harvested annually. A part of these are consumed while still green; nuts that are about nine months old contain a delicate jelly that is cherished here as a dessert. The remaining nuts are handcrafted into bowls and other vessels, or sold as they are to tourists. A unique souvenir, either burnished brown or in its natural grey state, but not exactly inexpensive (1988: between US$ 80 - 120). By the way, no two coco-de-mer are alike. It is said that their forms are as varied as those of their human, or rather female, counterparts. If you want a large selection to choose from, then ask for the government depot on Praslin, which is where all of the nuts are collected. To obtain an authentic nut in Mahé, look for the shop in Independence House, the entrance to which is found on 5th June Avenue. There are no special signs denoting its existence – except, that is, for a few coco-de-mer nuts in its display window.

Note: the Vallée de Mai presents itself in three distinct moods. So, if you have the time, plan to visit it on more than one occasion. The first mood can be experienced on dark and windy days when the palm leaves clash together, as described above, to produce a metallic sound. The second can be observed during sunny mornings, when the lush palm forest displays its endless shades of green in the interplay between light and shadow. The third takes place when there is a full moon, at which time the Vallée de Mai is transformed into an almost unearthly world of beauty and mystique. (Visiting the Vallée de Mai at various times of the day and night is no problem even if its hours are limited to 8 a.m. – 2:30 p.m. The road between Grand Anse and Baie Sainte Anne runs right through the centre of the park.)

Aldabra, Galapagos of the Indian Ocean

No matter which of the Seychelles' islands you stay on during your holiday, you will have the chance of seeing giant turtles in their natural environment or in reserves just about everywhere. And if you should happen to ask where these venerable animals might come from, the answer will almost always be: from Aldabra.

Where is this Aldabra? What is so special about the place? To put it succinctly: it is the remotest island of the archipelago, about 1,200 km (746 miles) southwest of the Seychelles' main island, Mahé, but only 400 km (249 miles) from Africa and 600 km (373 miles) from Madagascar. It developed some 80,000 years ago on the tip of a submerged volcano; today it is the largest coral atoll in the world. The entire island of Mahé would fit into its lagoon!

Furthermore, Aldabra is one of the most curious natural formations to be found anywhere on earth. It is a huge water basin, surrounded by mangroves. Water comes rushing in at high tide through four channels that resemble floodgates; at low tide the water recedes again, leaving the basin almost dry, with dead coral banks protruding the surface like huge mushrooms.

Aldabra's dry land area, only about 155 km^2 (60 mi^2) in size, turned out to be unsuitable for permanent settlement. A few settlers did arrive here in 1899 and planted some coconut

Giant tortoises, which originate in Aldabra, can be encountered at several Seychelles islands.

palms that can still be seen at a planta-tion on Grand Terre that extends for about 3 km. They also harvested fish and turtles from the sea. Nevertheless, the atoll was basically left as it had been for thousands of years: a wild and rough coral formation, particles of which cling tenaciously to clothes and skin; plagued by mosquitos and more reminiscent of a lunar landscape than a tropical island paradise.

Aldabra's inhospitable environment enhanced the development of a unique fauna. Competent scientists do not hesitate to compare Aldabra to the fa-mous Galapagos Islands, and that des-pite numerous differences. Both are ex-tremely important for the study of natural history and have animals that do not (or no longer) exist anywhere else and need to be protected. The two archipelagos are, for instance, the only two places in the world where

giant tortoises still live in freedom in such large numbers (about 8,000 in the Galapagos and some 150,000 on Aldabra, as of 1988).

And this despite the fact that things did not look so good for giant tortoises on Aldabra a short time ago. During the 19th century the island was re-peatedly invaded by parties in search of provisions: the tortoises represented a valuable source of protein, one which was readily available and could be stored live. Historical records show that in 1842 just two ships took on 1,200 of these animals. At the turn of the century it seemed as if the hour of doom was fast approaching for this species. An expedition had to search for three whole days before finding a single tortoise. Yet, there must still have been enough of them around, not only to be survive, but also to build up numbers again systematically. The government of the Seychelles deserves credit here for having imposed strict protective measures. It was supported in this effort by the UNESCO, which declared Aldabra one of mankind's great natural inheritances.

A more recent threat to the tortoise population of the Aldabra Atoll was recognized in good time and – with the help of naturalists from around the world – would seem to have been averted. The threat was posed by wild goats. Originally brought to the island by settlers, the goats soon grew wild and increased markedly in numbers. They not only competed with the tortoises for nourishment, but also consumed such quantities of leaves from both trees and shrubs that the tortoises were practically left without vital protection from the burning sun. Those concerned had to stand by as the tortoises were literally cooked in their own shells and died of dehydration.

Early in 1987 a programme was launched to reduce the number of goats. In the first phase, 200 were shot and then in the second phase, early in 1988, another 500. It is hoped that the remaining 200 goats (mid-1988) no longer pose an immediate threat. Should the opposite prove to be the case, the authorities are prepared to intervene once again.

Besides giant tortoises, there are a number of other animals that manage to survive on or around Aldabra. A great number of marine turtles come between December and March to lay their eggs on the beaches. Some 6,000 to 7,000 whitebreasted rail, a species which has lost the ability to fly, make their home here and nowhere else. Another endemic species of bird is the Aldabra stork with its porcelain-blue eyes. Sea birds, which populate the atoll by the thousands, include flamingos, herons and numerous representatives of tern and frigate birds, of which there are more in Aldabra than anywhere else in the Indian Ocean.

The government of the Seychelles has given the protection of Aldabra highest priority and has consequently prohibited the economic exploitation of the island. The only ones who will find ample "game" here are the scientists who come to study this natural wonder.

History of the Seychelles

Even historians disagree as to who really was the first to discover this group of islands in the middle of the Indian Ocean.

Most likely it was Arab merchants who sailed across the Indian Ocean about 1,000 years ago and first anchored their ships in the shallow waters of the Seychelles. Navigational charts dating back to the 9th century A.D. show a group of islands located to the south of the Maldives.

It is an established fact that Vasco da Gama discovered the Amirantes during his second circumnavigation of the world at the beginning of the 16th century. Today these islands are reckoned geographically as a part of the Seychelles archipelago. It is also known that the East India Company sent out an expedition in 1609 under the command of Alexander Sharpeigh to look for new trade markets and that, following navigational problems, his two ships, the "Ascension" and "Good Hope", dropped anchor off the Seychelles "by mere chance". Published logbooks of a later date report that seamen found ample supplies of coconuts, wood and fish, but never encountered any inhabitants during their forays into the islands' interiors. It seems, then, that the Seychelles were still uninhabited at this point.

A short time after, the French, who had already taken possession of the neighbouring island of Mauritius (for-merly known as Ile de France), discovered the secluded bays of Mahé, Praslin and La Digue. They made use of them as hideouts to escape the notice of pirates or as a base to repair their ships. But it may also have been a tactical manoeuvre on the part of Bertrand François Mahé de Labourdonnais, governor general of "Ile de France": by establishing the islands as naval bases he may well have thought to check the advances of the British fleet in the Indian Ocean.

In 1742 Mahé de Labourdonnais sent Captain Picault to the Seychelles, at which time the official history of the islands began to take its course. Nevertheless, another 14 years went by until, in 1756, the French captain Morphey installed the "Stone of Possession", raised the flag of his king Louis XV and named the islands in honour of that sovereign's minister of finance, Moreau de Séchelles.

The first French settlers came to the Seychelles in 1770, bringing their slaves with them. Following the French Revolution in 1789, the British thought they would have little trouble taking over the islands. But the commander of the island, Quéau de Quinssy, who had been appointed in 1794, tricked them. Seven times he struck down the flag as a sign of capitulation, only to raise it again just as soon as victorious British ships left Mahé's harbour.

His last capitulation in 1810, however, terminated this quaint interplay.

The Seychelles at a glance

Form of Government: Republic with a single-chamber parliament and one political party, the Seychelles Peoples Progressive Front (SPPF), which elects the president and governing ministers. France-Albert René has been head of state since 1977.

Territory: the total land area of the more than one hundred islands of the Seychelles is 443 km² (171 mi²); The islands are scattered over an area of some 400,000 km² (154,440 mi²) in the western Indian Ocean.

Population: named "Seychellois", including Negroes and mulattos, French Creoles and a minority of Indians, Chinese and Malays. Total: 66,300. Census according to island or island group: Mahé, 58,000; Praslin, 5,000; La Digue, 2,500; Silhouette, 250; other granite islands and Bird and Denis islands, 150; Amirantes, 250; Farquhar and Aldabra, 150 (end 1987).
  Language of the people since 1981: Creole; the languages of officialdom are English and French. Apart from Creole, which is spoken by the majority of the population, English is the most commom language.
  Religions: 91% of the population are Catholics, 7.5% are Anglicans; the remaining 1.5% belong to various religious communities.

Most important Exports: fish, copra, cinnamon, cinnamon oil, coconuts and guano. About 60% of foreign earnings are related to tourist activities. Main trading partners are: Great Britain, France and other members of the European Community, Pakistan, South Africa, Mauritius, Réunion, Kenya, the Peoples Republic of the Yemen, Japan, Singapore.

The British annexed the Seychelles and received permanent title to them in the Treaty of Paris in 1814.

The British recognized the capabilities and popularity of de Quinssy and suggested that the Frenchman remain in the Seychelles in their service. He accepted and showed his gratitude by changing his name to de Quincy (presently the name of a street in Mahé). For thirteen years, until 1827, he functioned as an intermediary between the French and British in the Seychelles. A fortunate act of providence that was to set the political tone on the island.

The liberation of the slaves in 1835 changed the islands' history markedly. The Seychelles became a refuge for many of those who had escaped from the maritime slave trade. A blend of races gradually took place and produced the typical Seychellois of today.

The next date of historical import was that of the Seychelles' transition to a British crown colony on August 31, 1903. Almost half a century of political inertia followed, during which the islands were also struck by economic problems resulting from isolation during World War I, the general depression of the twenties and thirties and World War II, when a number of Seychellois lost their lives.

Since 1964 the islands' political affairs have been in the hands of the Seychellois themselves. (Political parties and parliamentary elections had already been introduced under the British.) Over the following ten or more years the history of the Seychelles took another – hopefully final – turn. In 1965 the islands of Desroches (Amirantes), Aldabra and Farquhar were severed from the Seychelles and, together with the Chagos Archipelago (formerly a dependency of Mauritius), united to form the British Indian Ocean Territory. This colony – established under military considerations – existed in this form for just eleven years.

Aldabra, Farquhar and Desroches were returned to the Seychelles when the latter gained independence on June 29, 1976.

James R. Mancham was the first president of the Seychelles; he had held the office of prime minister under the British. France-Albert René has been president of the republic since 1977.

(Hedegaard)

History of the Seychelles at a glance

7th-10th century A.D. Islands presumably first visited by Arab traders.

15th/16th century. First mention of the Seychelles on Portuguese charts; Vasco da Gama discovers the Amirantes in 1502; João Nova discovers the Farquhar Atoll in 1504.

1609. A British East India Company expedition lands on the Seychelles.

17th/18th century. Pirates make use of the islands as hide-outs and supply bases.

1742. The Frenchman Lazare Picault lands on the Seychelles in the name of Francois Mahé de Labourdonnais, governor of the "Isle de France" (Mauritius), and gives the largest island the name "Ile d'Abondance".

1744. Lazare Picault is about again. On this journey he rechristens the "Ile d'Abondence", in honour of his governor, "Mahé".

1756. Captain Nicholas Morphey claims possession of the Seychelles in the name of his king, Louis XV, in honour of whose minister of finance the islands receive the name "Séychelles".

1770. The first French settlers and numerous slaves land on the island of St. Anne.

1772. A second settlement is founded, at Anse Royale on Mahé, to begin the cultivation of spices and vegetables.

1778. A third settlement on Mahé lays the foundation of what is to become the capital, Victoria.

1794. Quéau de Quinssy is appointed Governor of the Seychelles.

1794-1810. De Quinssy capitulates to British forces seven separate times.

1814. As provided for in the Treaty of Paris, the islands are ceded to the British Crown. The incumbent governor (under previous French rule) remains in office under the British until 1827.

1835. Slavery is abolished by act of the British Parliament.

1851. The first Catholic diocese is founded in Victoria.

1893. The first lines of communication to the outside world come into operation: a telegraph cable to Zanzibar and Mauritius.

1903. Administration of the Seychelles from Mauritius is terminated. The island is given the status of a British Crown Colony. The Seychelles, which had hitherto been made up of the so-called granite islands and the three coral islets of Denis, Ile aux Vaches (Bird) and Plate, were now given title to the islands of the Aldabra and Amirante archipelagos (with Alphonse), previously belonging to Mauritius.

1908. The island of Coëtivy (former territory of Mauritius) is appended to the Seychelles.

1911. The administration of the Seychelles ends its previous practice of classifying the islands' inhabitants according to race.

1916/17. Volunteer corps take part in campaigns in Africa and India.

1923. Victoria is supplied with electricity.

1932. The Farquhar Islands (formerly belonging to Mauritius) are turned over to the Seychelles.

1934. The Seychelles rupee becomes legal tender.

1948. Limited franchise is introduced. Election of a kind of "administrative council".

1959. The first merchant bank is established.

1964. Founding of the first political parties.

1965. The islands of Desroches (Amirantes), Aldabra and the Farquhar group become the British Indian Ocean Territory.

1970. The Seychelles are granted a degree of autonomy under Prime Minister Mancham.

1971. The international airport begins operations. Queen Elisabeth II attends the official opening ceremony the year following.

1976. The Seychelles are granted independence. James R. Mancham is nominated president and France-Albert René prime minister. The islands constituting the British Indian Ocean Territory since 1965 are returned.

1977. France-Albert René becomes president following a coup d'etat.

1979, 1984, 1989. France-Albert René is re-elected.

Location and Formation

Perhaps you can still recall the first time you saw photographs of the Seychelles in some magazine or brochure. Undoubtedly your attention was drawn by something other than the characteristic palms, white sand and blue waters of tropical "paradise": namely, the huge reddish boulders that often have unusual riffled polish to them and give the impression of having been created by some Hollywood set designer rather than nature. Well, the specialists in Hollywood obviously can't compete with millions of years of polishing work done by water, wind and sand. Otherwise they – and some renowned fashion photographers – wouldn't take the trouble to come here and use the colourful granite boulders of the Seychelles for their beach scenes.

Picture-book beaches with such typical boulders have become a sort of trademark of the Seychelles or, to be more precise, of the so-called granite islands that rise up from a 20,000-km² (7,722-mi²) granite base, the Mahé Plateau. These are the islands most frequented by tourists; they tower above the sea like the tips of submerged mountains and some reach respectable heights. The island of Mahé, for instance, rises up to 905 metres (2,970 feet) above sea level, while the smaller isles of Praslin and La Digue attain a height of 340 and 333 metres (1,115 and 1,093 feet) respectively. The mountain slopes are usually quite steep, especially on Mahé. The bare rock glistens through the dense vegetation over wide patches along the slopes; the "glacis", or sloping rock face, is broken up by deep ravines and sheer cliffs. There are no true rivers, but hundreds of brooks cascade down the slopes. Flat, arable land is a scarce commodity on all of the granite islands; most of it is found in the form of relatively thin stretches along the coast that are frequently interrupted by bodies of water or swampy areas. Mangroves and beaches line the shores of the islands, but granite cliffs or boulders often extend into the sea.

The granite found on Mahé, Praslin, La Digue and a number of other smaller islands, is one of the world's oldest rock formations. It dates back to the Precambian and is thus some 650 million years old! The syenite and microsyenite found on Silhouette and North Island are of more recent rigin, probably from the Tertiary period. The seabed surrounding the islands is made up of layers of fossilized coral; these have formed protective reefs in places. Coral islands only formed along the northern rim of the Mahé Plateau. Bird and Denis are the closest islands of this type (i.e. closest in relation to Mahé). In the vicinity of these two islands, the shallow waters of the Mahé Plateau (averaging between 30-60 metres/99-197 feet in depth) empty into the depths of the Indian Ocean, plunging to more than 1,800 metres (5,900 feet) – which is why the islands are also a prime deep-sea fishing area.

All other Seychelles islands located outside the Mahé Plateau are coral atolls, the largest being Aldabra. There are more of these than granite isles: the ratio is about 55 coral to 40 granite islands. Establishing exact figures is unrealistic in this case, as some of the tiny isles – actually more like sandbanks or offshore boulders – may or may not be included in official statistics. Then again, exact figures are really not that important since they say little about the actual extension of the Seychelles, which is truly remarkable. Whereas the coral islands of the Amirantes archipelago, some 300 km (186 miles) away, can be viewed as being fairly close to Mahé, distances become quite impressive in the case of the Farquhar group (800 km/497 miles) and even more so with the Aldabra islands (1,100 km/684 miles).

On the other hand, it is only about 650 km (404 miles) from Aldabra to the coast of Tanzania in Africa and the Farquhar archipelago is a mere 400 km (249 miles) away from the northern tip of the island of Madagascar.

The assumption that the Seychelles may at some time have been connected to Madagascar, the closest larger landmass, is generally rejected by geologists. For one, the granite Mahé Plateau is part of the Mascarene Ridge, which makes a wide arch beneath the sea of some 2,500 km (1,550 miles) in extension in the direction of the islands of Mauritius and Réunion – and not Madagascar. Furthermore scientists find it more probable that the Seychelles once formed part of a sub-continent joining Africa and Asia, or that they remained as fragments following the continental shift between Africa and India.

Whatever the case may be, it is certain that the isolated position of the Seychelles for millions of years ensured the survival of ancient land and life forms hardly found elsewhere on earth. Many a scientist will not shy away from equating the Seychelles with the Galapagos Islands as far as their importance in evolutionary history is concerned. More of this in another chapter.

Climate, Weather Conditions, Best Times to Visit

A long flight, then the request that passengers remain seated while the interior of the aircraft is disinfected - time consuming, yes, but a precautionary measure and one laid down by the Seychelles authorities. Finally the word is given to disembark. At long last a breath of fresh air...and new arrivals to the Seychelles are either shocked or enchanted. Shocked by the apparent humidity which engulfs them or enchanted by the glorious tropical warmth which seems to announce "Holiday at last!"

Both sensations are perfectly normal since people's reactions to climatic changes are usually as varied as the people themselves. Added to this comes the fact that the body must adapt to the radical transition from the relatively cool and (inevitably) very dry air inside the aeroplane and the humid atmosphere of the tropics.

Most people need two or three days to acclimatize; the length of time will also depend upon your point of departure. For Europeans the process is not particularly problematic since the time difference between Europe and the Seychelles is only minimal (G.M.T. + 4 hours, Central European time + 3 hours; this compares favourably with the up to 6 hours difference between Europe and the holiday islands of the Caribbean or Southeast Asia). Visitors from the Americas face more problems with jet lag.

The main holiday islands of the Seychelles, i.e. the granite islands of the Mahé group, lie just beneath the equator (4° south latitude). In the light of this, visitors here can expect fairly constant climatic conditions all year round. In terms of facts and figures, the mean annual temperature is 26.7°C (80°F) with only marginal deviations between an average 26.2°C (79°F) in July and 27.7°C (almost 82°F) in May. Relative atmospheric humidity remains between 77% and 83% on average and is therefore noticeably lower than in other tropical regions. This, together with the cooling breezes which blow steadily except when there is a reversal of monsoon direction (April/May and October/November), makes for a pleasant tropical maritime climate, one especially appreciated by visitors from more northerly climes.

The climate of the Seychelles is determined to a significant degree by the monsoons. These seasonal winds (they change direction on a half yearly basis) are caused by pressure gradients created by the warming (and cooling) of a large landmass (Asia) and an extensive area of water (the Indian Ocean). So it is that we find two distinct sets of climatic conditions in the Seychelles:

✦ the cooler, drier season, with the southeast monsoon beginning in May and abating in October;
✦ the hotter, more humid season from November well into March when the northwest monsoon blows.

Between these two seasons we find the transitional periods mentioned above. Distinguished by spells of absolute calm and the very high temperatures associated with them, these transitional periods are seen by some as uncomfortably hot and oppressive and by others as quite simply the ideal time for a stay on the islands.

The onset of the northwest monsoon also means the beginning of the rainy season. It would perhaps be more accurate to say the period of more plentiful rainfall since precipitation does occur all year round but is more frequent and abundant during the northwest monsoon, when showers are more sudden, at times squally and often of much longer duration. With any luck you'll only experience such heavy and extended showers at night – or rather, you won't experience them at all because you'll be asleep. But even if you do have to seek shelter from the rain - and even should you be soaked at some point – don't allow this to dampen the holiday spirit. Rain in the Seychelles is pleasantly warm and is not accompanied by the cool winds familiar to most of us in temperate zones. What's more, in the tropical summer warmth you are bound to be wearing light, airy clothing, which means that a shower will soak you to the skin almost immediately...but that you'll dry off again almost as quickly.

Since the northwest monsoon in the Seychelles coincides with winter in the northern hemisphere, the period between November and March represents the islands' high season. Visitors can revel in the prospect of seeing the islands literally burst into life when, as of November, the first rains bring out the vegetation in force: splashes of brilliantly-coloured blossoms, lush greenery and a heightened sense of joie de vivre in both man and beast. Those aiming to capture their Seychelles experience on film will be especially enthralled by the "photogenic" clouds which are a regular feature at this time of year. Hotel guests along the west coast of Mahé, and particularly on Beau Vallon Bay, will be less enthusiastic when strong winds mean rough seas and dangerous surf (breaking on the beaches, it can leave seaweed behind).

Climatic Table Mahé/Victoria (Airport)

Month	Daily high		Nightly low		Daily hours of sunshine	Humidity in %	No.of days with rain	Rainfall in mm
	°C	°F	°C	°F				
January	29	84	24	75	6	83	22	380
February	29	84	25	77	6	77	15	230
March	30	86	25	77	7	78	16	250
April	30	86	25	77	8	80	15	180
May	31	88	25	77	8	79	14	200
June	28	82	25	77	7	79	14	100
July	27	81	24	75	7	81	12	100
August	27	81	24	75	7	81	11	150
September	28	82	24	75	7	81	12	150
October	28	82	24	75	7	83	13	250
November	29	84	24	75	7	83	17	350
December	29	84	24	75	6	82	20	350

When it comes time for the southeast monsoon to take over, it is the guests of east coast hotels who bear the brunt of the wind. This is generally stronger and more constant, in particular in the period from June to August, and therefore ensures excellent sport for windsurfers (providing they have reached a fair degree of proficiency on their boards). Notwithstanding strong winds, the whole length of Mahé's east coast is extremely dry when compared with other parts of the island. This is because the east coast is quite a distance (relatively speaking) from the mountains which generate relief rainfall in their vicinity.

The mountainous islands do register a higher level of rainfall annually. At altitude on Mahé, rainfall can in fact reach 2,800 mm/110 ins yearly (as opposed to just 1,600 mm/63 ins at Anse Royale in the southeast of the island). But it isn't only altitude which affects precipitation on Mahé: rainfall also increases irrespective of this as one moves northwards. Two figures to illustrate this: Anse Boileau at the southwest coast records some 1,800 mm/70 ins rainfall annually; Bel Ombre up on the northwest coast sees almost 2,500 mm/98 ins.

And the best time to visit? For those who prefer cooler, drier and breezier conditions, the period between May and October is definitely to be recommended (although it must be said that July and August see a large number of visitors). Those who like temperatures to be high (and who are not averse to some rain and to the higher levels of atmospheric humidity associated with both) should opt for the season December to March (most visitors come between mid-December and mid-January). For those who yearn peace and quiet, and who are fairly flexible in holiday arrangements, April/May and October/November may prove quite a boon: there will be far fewer guests in hotels and hardly a breath of wind to stir the palm trees or ruffle the sea. Temperatures will be higher – to the delight of some, to the dismay of others – and it may become quite humid at times.

As for the other islands, the picture is very varied. At higher elevations on Silhouette (the island reaches an altitude of some 750 m/2,460 ft), rainfall stands at about 2,000 mm/79 ins annually. Praslin and La Digue reach only about half the altitude of Silhouette but record rainfall of 1,900 mm/75 ins and 1,500 mm/59 ins respectively. These figures correspond roughly with precipitation levels at similar elevations (i.e. less than 1,000 m) in Central Europe, the only difference being that on the granite islands of the Seychelles precipitation is concentrated in the period from November to January.

The low-lying coral islands of the group, e.g. Bird Island and Denis Island, register just a little over half the rainfall occurring on Mahé. On the Outer Islands the figure is even lower, in some places much lower.

A few closing remarks on the subject of climate: the Seychelles lie outside the cyclone belt, which means that violent storms are extremely rare occurrences; the sun rises at much the same time all year – around 6.30 a.m. – and sets just as regularly at 6.30 p.m. after a brief twilight; the temperature of the sea, a constant 26-30°C (79-86°F), makes for pleasant bathing all year.

ABC of Islands and Beaches

More than 100 islands of the Seychelles have been registered by name. To list them all here, to say nothing of describing them, would probably confuse rather than be of service to you. Only about a quarter of them are suitable for a visit, whether your sojourn be long or short. But even here one has to be selective with a view to touristic infrastructure. Some of the islands are well worth a visit, but offer neither accommodation nor acceptable means of transportation. Others are only accessible for scientific research or are in private hands and thus closed off to visitors.

There are two reasons why the following list does not strictly adhere to alphabetical order. Firstly, the principal island of Mahé has been given priority over others and, secondly, the islands have been divided into two groups, just as the Seychellois themselves are wont to do: the so-called Inner Islands and Outer Islands. Included among the former are the granite islands and the two coral islands (Bird and Denis) on the Seychelles Bank, the central underwater plateau. These will normally be the islands where you spend your vacation. The term "Outer Islands" refers to those islands that are located off the Seychelles Bank, somewhere in the expanses of the Indian Ocean: i.e. the coral islands of the Amirantes, Farquhar and Aldabra groups. Desroches, the largest of the Amirantes has been accessible to tourists since April 1988. As it is less likely that you will reach any of the other Outer Islands during your stay, these are only described in brief here.

Most of the Seychelles' beaches bear the French name of "Anse", which means "small bay". This gives you a notion already of what kind of beaches to expect: with few exceptions, they will be relatively small, gently curved, bordered by bizarre granite formations and almost always lined with tropical trees such as coconut palms, takamaka or casuarina. The quality of the beaches is definitely top rate: fine, white sand that has not yet been affected by pollution (except, perhaps, the kind tourists may leave behind). The same can be said as far as the water is concerned: clear, clean and only occasionally slightly murky at some beaches (e.g. Beau Vallon Bay) when the seas are rough and the sand is churned up.

A few beaches are said to be periodically infested with sand fleas. Actually, these are sand flies that appear sporadically here and there at certain times of the year or when particular weather conditions prevail. Unfortunately none of the local inhabitants seem to be able to tell just exactly when this happens. Even then, some people will be afflicted and others not at all. At any rate, the tiny bites are not dangerous to your health. They just itch unpleasantly.

That can be avoided by using insect repellent and by using a towel whenever you want to lie down on the beach.

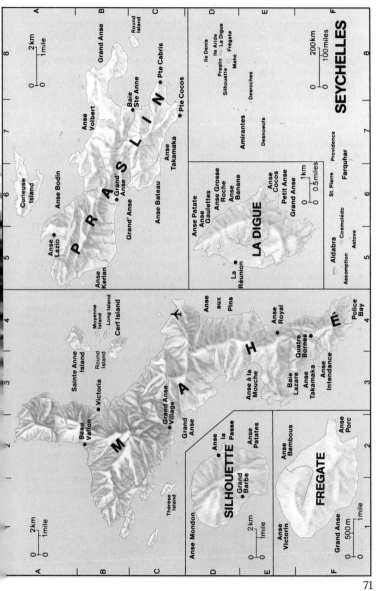

SEYCHELLES

MAHÉ

- Anse Mondon
- Sainte Anne Island
- Round Island
- Moyenne Island
- Long Island
- Cerf Island
- Thérèse Island
- Beau Vallon
- Victoria
- Grand Anse Village
- Grand Anse
- Anse aux Pins
- Anse Royal
- Anse à la Mouche
- Baie Lazare
- Anse Takamaka
- Anse Intendance
- Quatre Bornes
- Police Bay

PRASLIN

- Curieuse Island
- Grand Anse
- Round Island
- Anse Lazio
- Anse Bodin
- Anse Kerlan
- Grand' Anse
- Grand' Anse
- Anse Volbert
- Baie Ste Anne
- Pte Cabris
- Anse Takamaka
- Anse Bateau
- Pte Cocos

LA DIGUE

- Anse Patate
- Anse Gaulettes
- Anse Grosse Roche
- Anse Banane
- Anse Cocos
- Petit Anse
- Grand Anse
- La Réunion

SILHOUETTE

- Anse la Passe
- Grand Barbe
- Anse Patates

FREGATE

- Anse Porc
- Anse Bambous
- Anse Victorin
- Grand Anse

SEYCHELLES

- Ile Denis
- Ile Aride
- Praslin
- La Digue
- Silhouette
- Mahé
- Frégate
- Amirantes
- Desroches
- Desnoeufs
- St. Pierre
- Providence
- Farquhar
- Aldabra
- Assomption
- Cosmolédo
- Astove

71

Details of individual beaches have been listed under the corresponding islands in order to avoid confusion, as the names often repeat themselves. There is, for instance, a beach called "Grand Anse" on Mahé, as well as on Praslin, La Digue and Frégate.

Inner Islands

Mahé will undoubtedly be the place where you first set foot on Seychelles ground. Being the principal island, on which the capital city of Victoria is located, it also has the only international airport and the only harbour capable of servicing ocean liners. But it stands out from among the other islands in many more ways:
✦ about 90% of the total population of the Seychelles lives on Mahé;
✦ the capital, Victoria, has about 25,000 inhabitants (out of a total population of the islands of 66,300 – 1987/88) and is thus the main area of urbanization;
✦ most of the tourist hotels are found on Mahé, which boasts about 85% of the total bedding capacity;
✦ with its mountainous interior - the Mornes reach altitudes over 600 metres (1,970 feet) and the peak of

Morne Seychellois a proud 905 metres (2,970 feet) - Mahé offers the widest range of scenic contrasts, from exotic beaches to tropical alpine forests;
✦ Mahé has the most extensive and best road network;
✦ on Mahé the tourist will find the widest selection of sports facilities, entertainment and excursions - due to its central location, Mahé is the best place from which to go "island hopping".

North Mahé is characterized by a gently sloping coastline on the east side and a hilly and rocky western coast that sometimes drops steeply into the sea to form several small coves. The west coast carries over into the bay of Beau Vallon, which is undoubtedly the most important coastal strip on Mahé in terms of tourism: about a third of the island's bedding capacity is found there.

Central Mahé, site of the Morne Seychellois, is dominated on its eastern side by the capital Victoria and a group of offshore islands made up of Ste. Anne, Moyenne, Cerf, Round and Long Island. The western coastline is fairly rough and inaccessible in some places.

South Mahé makes up the flatter part of the island, although parts of it still reach an altitude of 500 metres (1,640 feet). The coastline, which is broken up into numerous coves, still lacks a touristic infrastructure and is thus fairly pristine.

Victoria, the capital city, with its 15,000 inhabitants (about 25,000 if we include the densely populated sub-

A fine example of old colonial architecture: the restored plantation house in "Village Artisanale".

urbs), is proud to be known as one of the "smallest capitals of the world". Indeed, village charm more aptly describes the situation here than metropolitan flair.

The centre of this little city is small and easy to negotiate. All of Victoria's special attractions and attributes are found within a radius of about 500 metres from its axis, the clock tower which is known locally as "L'Horloge". Streets leading away from it have the best shopping facilities: take, for example, Independence Avenue and the Victoria Arcades in Victoria House. This is where most of the banks, travel agencies and airlines have their offices; the national museum and the main post office are also located here.

The local inhabitants prefer doing their shopping on Market Street, where the market gets busy at sunrise, or around 5:30 a.m., every Saturday. The many shops, most of them owned by East Indians, also draw the attention of keen shoppers, offering as they do just about everything a Seychellois family may need. Tucked away in the narrow alleys are also numerous photogenic old houses.

Heading northward, it is worthwhile to visit the Capuchin House (with its Portuguese flair) and the Cathedral of the Immaculate Conception (with the belltower behind it). To the east, the old and new harbour (latter is a land reclamation project of the 60's) provide one with interesting impressions. If you decide to head southward towards

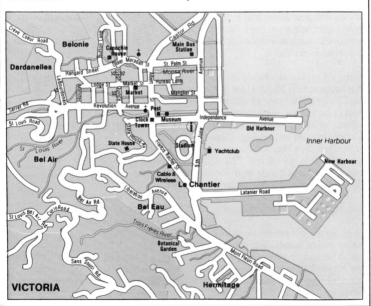

the Botanical Garden (absolutely recommendable!), then do have a look at the old Cable & Wireless building (next to its present-day counterpart) on Francis Rachel Street. The white colonial structure dating back to 1893 has been carefully restored; it lies hidden behind a high hedge.

If you have seen all these, then you have come to know the main points of interest for visitors in all of Victoria!

Excursions on Mahé are more practicable than on other islands. Various possibilities, including destinations, tours and means of transportation, are described in the chapter "Out and About in the Seychelles" (p.130).

All of **68 beaches on Mahé** make the choice of which to visit rather difficult. Listed below are the most important ones, going in a clockwise direction from Beau Vallon.

Beau Vallon is undoubtedly the best-known beach on Mahé. Here one will find the greatest range of accommodation (3 hotels) and water sports facilities, including windsurfing, sailing, paragliding and waterskiing. The latter is best between May and November, when the seas are calmest. The white beach extends in a wide arch, for three kilometres; it is framed by mountains and lined with takamaka trees and palms. (Northwestern coast)

Anse Royal, not behind Beau Vallon in either size or beauty, is preferred by many because there are no hotels and the snorkelling between shore and reef is even better here. Many Seychellois come up here with their families at

weekends to picnic. During the week, however, one will encounter very few people. Fishermen dock their boats near the village of Anse Royale; they can be seen bringing in their catch in the mornings or late afternoons. (Southern coast)

Police Bay, one of the more isolated and less-frequented beaches on Mahé, with granite configuration that correspond to the ideal image of the Seychelles. A strong surf makes it that much more photogenic - but careful when swimming! (Southwestern coast)

Anse Intendance, similar to Police Bay, only longer and wider, and thus perhaps Mahé's most beautiful beach. Swimmers need to watch out for hazardous currents. (Southwestern coast)

Anse Takamaka has more palms than its name suggests. It is a quickly sloping beach with much wave action and currents, especially between May and October. (Southwestern coast)

Baie Lazare was named after Lazare Picault, who arrived in Mahé in 1742 with the first French expedition. This beach also forms a steep cove and is further protected by a massive granite rock formation. Snorkelling is good here and numerous trees provide welcome shade. A good portion of the beach is part of the complex of the Hotel Plantation Club. (Southwestern coast)

Anse à la Mouche is the name of a narrow cove with palm-lined shoreline and still waters. It becomes quite shallow at low tide. (Southwestern coast)

Grand Anse stretches for about 2 km (over a mile) and is thus one of Mahé's longest beaches. As there are no hotels directly alongside, only in the vicinity, it is relatively unfrequented. High waves, especially between November and April, make it an ideal place for surfers. Unpredictable currents, however, can be hazardous for swimmers. Takamaka trees predominate here rather than palms. (Western coast)

Aride Island, northernmost of the granite islands, lies about 60 km (37 miles) north of Mahé and 10 km (6 miles) north of Praslin. It rises 152 metres (500 feet) out of crystal-clear waters and is partially surrounded by a coral reef. The name "Aride" (= dry) is misleading: the island is covered with lush vegetation. Its topsoil is made of the excrements of millions of seabirds that have lived on the island for an equal number of years.

The island was private property for about one hundred years and the rigorous exploitation of birds' eggs brought it close to an ecological collapse. It was purchased in 1973 by Cadbury, the British chocolate producer, and entrusted to the Society for the Promotion of Nature Conservation. Since then, Aride has had a de facto status as a nature reserve and allowing the island to recuperate - without human intervention - has become the primary goal.

With ten species that brood here, Aride has the largest colony of sea birds within the region of the granite isles. There are more representatives of the common noddy and roseate

tern here than anywhere else in the world. But there are also numerous great frigate birds and red-tailed tropic birds. The flora has some interesting botanical highlights, such as Wright's gardenia, or bois citron, a bush with white blossoms that only grows on Aride.

When the southeasterly monsoon winds blow (primarily between May and September), rough seas make landing on the island much too dangerous for tourists and trips are consequently not possible. And, indeed, even during the more "appropriate" season (between October and April) there are still days on which tourist boats simply cannot reach the island. Those who are interested should definitely sign up for the trip ahead of time at one of the agencies in Mahé or their representatives at hotels in Praslin. That way one can be assured of a passage as soon as weather conditions permit (duration of the trip from Mahé is about 2 $1/2$ to 3 hours; from Praslin about $3/4$ to 1 hour). Landing fee for Aride: SR 75 per person.

Bird Island. Another major bird sanctuary of the Inner Islands, but of a distinctive character: it is a flat, palm-covered coral island. Privately owned, Bird Island is located just under 100 km (60 miles) north of Mahé and can be reached in about 40 minutes by plane. Great numbers of fairy terns and common noddies live here permanently, as well as barred ground doves, Madagascar fodies and lapwings. But the most impressive natural spectacle has to be the flocks of millions of sooty terns that come here to brood around April/May and remain until October/November to raise their young. Their brooding grounds cover the northern part of the island and begin just a few hundred metres from the island's lodge. A lookout platform offers a good view of the brooding area.

A regular biological sensation on Bird Island comes in shape of the two giant tortoises living there, one of which, "Esmeralda" (a male tortoise, by the way), is said, at over 150 years of age, to be the oldest, largest and heaviest tortoise in the world.

The white coral beaches are ideal for swimming, snorkelling and shell collecting. The waters around Bird Island, which reach a profundity of about 1,800 metres (5,900 feet) along the steep Seychelles Bank, are prime sites for deep-sea fishermen.

Local travel agencies arrange daily excursions by plane from Mahé with at least one overnight stay. If you would like to combine a holiday on Mahé with a few days' sojourn on Bird Island, you should book a complete package with your own travel agent at home. The Bird Island Lodge has 25 separate and airy bungalows, as well as the usual amenities. Those who decide to remain for a few days will get a much more vivid impression of the nature spectacle on Bird Island.

Cerf Island forms part of the Ste. Anne Marine National Park and lies about 5 km (3 miles) east of Mahé's coast. This tiny, verdant island is populated by a few families who make a living by raising fruits and vegetables, as well as harvesting coconuts for sale. A quaint restaurant here is noted for its creole cooking and is thus a popular noontime stopover for boat excursions.

Cousin Island is one of the main bird sanctuaries of the granite isles, second in importance only to Aride. The island was purchased in 1968 by the International Council for Bird Preservation in order to protect rare and endangered species of land and sea birds. Thus the brush warbler has been assured a permanent habitat here as well as turtle doves, white-tailed tropic birds, wedge-tailed shearwaters and several species of tern. It is estimated that about 250,000 birds live on this 25-hectare (62-acre) island with a diameter of just one kilometre. The coral reef that almost completely encloses the island boasts 30 identified species of coral and 230 species of fish, thus being one of the Seychelles' richest marine environments.

For 30 years now, it has been prohibited to interfere in any way with the natural processes on the island. This has meant that the original deciduous forest has had a chance to recover and presently provides birds with a proper brooding environment. Another factor that has enhanced the preservation of the bird population is that predators like cats and rats have been successfully kept off the island.

Unlike Aride, Cousin Island is fairly accessible. Nevertheless, averse wind or tidal conditions can make the passage through the coral reef difficult, if not impossible.

In order not to disturb the birds excessively, the number of visitors is limited and visits are only allowed on the island on three days of the week: normally on Tuesdays, Thursdays and Fridays. Tours embark from Grand Anse on Praslin and are organized by local travel agencies as well as the hotels Indian Ocean Fishing Club and Maison des Palmes. It costs SR 50 to land on Cousin Island (the fee includes a 2-hour guided tour); the hotels charge as much again for the trip over and back.

Cousine Island, Cousin's "sister island", is privately owned and not accessible to the public.

Curieuse Island is separated from Praslin by a narrow strait approximately one mile in width. Formerly Curieuse held a leper colony and the ruins of the leprosarium, abandoned in 1965, can be visited along with the surrounding housing facilities. Other than the families of a few keepers, the island is uninhabited. Several hundred giant tortoises have been living here for a few years; they were brought over from Aldabra, where they were raised in an effort to increase the stock. Curieuse Marine National Park, named after the island, has a somewhat different marine flora and fauna than its counterpart, Ste. Anne. Tours - also in conjunction with a visit to Cousin - are arranged by hotels on Praslin. (See also the chapter "The Seychelles and Conservation" p.152)

Denis Island, like its close neighbour Bird Island, is a small and flat coral isle on the edge of the Seychelles Bank. It is about 80 km (50 miles) away from Mahé and can be reached by plane in approximately 35 minutes. Parts of the island are covered with a thick canopy of palms, takamakas and casuarinas; other parts are used agriculturally (vegetables, fruit, copra, livestock). Giant tortoises inhabit the island along with its owners and several Seychellois families. Marine turtles occasionally crawl up the beaches to lay their eggs. There are two long beaches located on opposite sides of the island; this has the advantage that one or the other is always on the lee side of the monsoon, which changes direction every six months. Thus the conditions for swimming, snorkelling, windsurfing or sailing are ideal the whole year round. Denis is also considered to be a prime site for deep-sea fishing. Wahoos, barracudas and tuna are caught throughout the year, while the season for black and blue marlin is between October/November and April/May.

Denis has all of the characteristics of an "unspoilt" holiday resort; 24 bungalows are available for a limited number of guests only. The concept of the French owners, the Burkhardts, is to provide their guests with a quiet and relaxing refuge, coupled with an atmosphere of cultivated hospitality. Day-trippers are therefore not catered to; instead, a sojourn of at least five days is expected (can be booked at your travel agents's, also in connection with stays on other islands).

A rather curious anecdote: in order that his guests take better advantage of daylight hours (and evenings), Mr. Burkhardt has established a special time zone for Denis Island - Mahé time plus one hour!

Felicité, a tiny island of no more than 3 km^2 (0.7 mi^2) located 3 km (1.8

miles) east of La Digue, is covered with lush tropical vegetation that often grows right down to the shore. Various trails cross its mountainous interior; snorkelling is great roundabout its coastline. Its population is made up of about a dozen individuals who subsist thanks to copra production, agriculture and fishing. A small hotel (3 rooms) is run by the La Digue Island Lodge.

Frégate Island is the easternmost of the granite islands, about 60 km (37 miles; 15 flight minutes) from Mahé. More so than any other island of the Seychelles, Frégate exudes the atmosphere of a faraway paradise that has been lavishly endowed by nature.

Just a few paces behind the plantation house, which is towered over by a huge banyan tree, begins a thick jungle that becomes impenetrable further inland. About 100 giant tortoises live here as well as a number of rare land birds, such as the magpie robin. It is only found on Frégate , where it can be observed in close company with the giant tortoises.

Several trails lead through the island's interior, which is dominated by the 125-metre (410-foot) Mt. Signale. These trails are a real treat for friends of tropical flora and fauna; unfortunately, they are not always easily recognizable. The five exceptionally beautiful beaches with their granite and palm backgrounds also have to be reached on foot: <u>Anse Bambous</u> in the north and <u>Anse Parc</u> in the southeast in about a 10-minute walk; <u>Anse Victorin</u> in the northwest (especially recommendable) in about 1/2 hour. The best places to go snorkelling (only at

high tide) are <u>Anse Parc</u> and <u>Grand Anse</u>.

In former times Frégate was used by pirates as a hideaway and supply base. Today, several Seychellois families keep busy planting fruit, coffee, spices and sugarcane - not only to cover their own needs, but also those of the guests staying at the plantation house and its two dependencies. As Air Seychelles now offers two daily flights (morning and afternoon) to and from Mahé, the island of Frégate is becoming an increasingly popular destination for one-day tours.

La Digue is, as far as its life style (and not its geographical location) is concerned, one of the "remotest" of the Inner Islands. There are few motorized vehicles available for the approximately 2,500 inhabitants; the main means of transportation are the ox cart and the bicycle. A bus line has been in operation along the west coast since 1988, but demand for its services is so low that it remains to be seen whether it can maintain itself.

The island itself has the appearance of a large palm grove with many old plantation houses standing along its paths. There is also a traditional copra

mill as well as a protected area specifically for the black paradise flycatcher, which only nests on La Digue. Strange rock formations crop up here and there along the coast and the interior, where they sometimes attain heights of 333 metres (over 1,000 feet). Occasionally they also form the extremes of sandy coves; then the single or stacked colossal blocks of granite produce the typical Seychelles seascape. This is particularly true of the southeastern part of the island: take, for example, Grand Anse, Petit Anse and Anse Cocos. Here, however, rough seas and treacherous currents can pose a hazard for swimmers. At the longest beach, Anse la Réunion, which is protected by a coral reef, bathing can sometimes be impeded by plant growth in the water, especially at low tide. One of the scenically most beautiful beaches is Anse Patates, located in the north: tall waves crash down upon the white sand and mighty red granite boulders. Snorkelling and bathing are ideal at Anse Gaulettes, Anse Grosse Roche and Anse Banane, in the still, shallow waters between shore and reef. But this is not to say that the areas beyond the reefs – and, indeed, the waters all around La Digue – are not ideally suited to snorkelling and scuba diving, too. There, one encounters a unique marine landscape between granite rock formations.

All beaches on La Digue can be reached quite easily by bicycle from the few hotels and guest houses situated along the western coast. For those staying at the island's largest hotel, La Digue Island Lodge, it is possible to charter a bus (if there are enough prospective passengers) for trips to beaches like Grand Anse (SR 30), as well as for tours of the island that include stops at Belle Vue, where one has a panoramic view of La Digue and Praslin, and the beaches along the east coast, all the way to Anse Banane (SR 100).

Day-trippers from Mahé usually fly to Praslin and then join the vacationers there to embark on the ferry crossing to La Digue. Tours by boat to and from Mahé, which usually include both Praslin and La Digue, should only be considered during fair weather, and then only by those who are seaworthy, as wind and waves can pick up at any time.

Long Island forms part of the Ste. Anne Marine National Park. This "Alcatraz of the Seychelles" is not open to the public.

Moyenne Island is also located within the Ste. Anne Marine National Park and gives one the impression of a lush tropical garden. This is due in part to the efforts of the owner of this 25-acre island, who has planted some 5,000 trees since 1973, including casuarina, sandragon and even a few coco-de-mer. He also laid out a path around the island with panoramic views of the neighbouring islands and leading past an old Creole house (with a few Museum pieces) and a chapel that stands by two pirate graves. This is also where the owner's father, Brendon Grimshaw, was laid to rest in 1987.

To sit on the shady veranda of the "Jolly Roger Bar" and listen to Grimshaw's yarns and ghost stories is a real pleasure. But one can also enjoy the natural environment, the birds and the giant tortoises of Moyenne, not to mention swimming or snorkelling in its warm, shallow waters. (See also "Mr. Grimshaw and the Ghosts of Moyenne", p.40).

A visit to Moyenne usually takes place in conjunction with a boat tour of the Ste. Anne Marine National Park and will invariably include a lunch after one has taken a walk around the island. It is also possible to stay there for an extended period, but arrangements have to be made in Mahé.

North Island lies about 30 km (17 miles) to the northwest of Mahé and 6 km (4 miles) north of Silhouette. It is a rocky island rising up to an altitude of 214 metres (700 feet), and therefore only partially farmed by its approximately 80 inhabitants. Fruit and vegetables are playing an increasingly important role here, along with palm products.

North Island was the first of the Seychelles islands to be visited by Europeans: the expedition under Alexander Sharpleigh arrived here in 1609. Today visitors usually book a day's tour from Victoria at one of the local travel agencies.

Praslin is the second largest island of the archipelago after Mahé; it extends for about 12 km (7 miles) in length and 5 km (3 miles) in width. Its approximately 5,000 inhabitants subsist primarily on agriculture and fishing. It is dominated by several mountain ranges that rise up to 340 metres (1,115 feet) in the western part of the island and enclose the Vallée de Mai to the east, a national park and last natural environment of the famous coco-de-mer (this botanical rarity has been described in several places, e.g. in "Highlights", "Flora" and in the chapter "Coco-de-Mer, Fruit from the Sea").

If you are spending your vacation on Mahé, a mere 40 km (25 miles) away, you should definitely plan to visit Praslin and the Vallée de Mai. This entails a boat trip of only 2 hours each way or an island hop by air of 15 minutes; both can be arranged with local travel agencies.

But Praslin is also well worth a longer stay, perhaps in combination with Mahé and even if only to enjoy its large or small beaches, which are bound to be relatively unfrequented.

The beaches along the west coast stretch for many kilometres (sometimes becoming quite narrow) from Anse Kerlan past the bay of Grand Anse, via Anse Bateau and Anse Takamaka, all the way to Pte. Cocos, the southernmost spot on the island. As there are few hotels or bungalows in Grand Anse, the beaches are usually empty of people. Sometimes, however, swimming here is not exactly a pleasure as loose sand and marine plants get tossed around the shore. This happens primarily during the northwest monsoon.

The hotels, bungalows and guest houses on the east coast are spaced at wide intervals along the somewhat shorter, but that much wider, beach of Anse Volbert, also called Côte d'Or. Here one will find the widest variety of sports facilities, especially for sailing, windsurfing and snorkelling. The beaches of the west and east coasts mentioned above tend to incline gradually seawards and remain shallow all the way out to the fairly distant reefs.

In the northern part of Praslin there is Anse Lazio, praised by connoisseurs as the most beautiful of the "granite beaches". Although its location is quite remote, it is becoming less and less peaceful because the narrow and rather poor road from Anse Boudin is currently being used by motorists as well as cyclists. On windy days during the northwest monsoon season, Anse Lazio can show the rougher side of its demeanour - it lacks a protective reef.

At the opposite end of the island, right on top of a hill located just above Pte. Cabris, there is an establishment which gourmets avow to be the "culinary hub" of the Seychelles: the exclusive "Chateau de Feuilles".

If you really want to get to know Praslin "from the inside", you should either bike or hike along the trails and paths that are closed off to motorized vehicles (see also "Sports in the Seychelles", p.141).

As far as excursions from Praslin are concerned, there are essentially four tours to be recommended: to the neighbouring islands of La Digue, Cousin, Aride and Curieuse. Just what you can see or do there is described in the sections dedicated to said islands in this chapter.

Praslin's airport was improved technically and its runway extended in June 1988, so that it is now possible for larger craft to land both during the day and at night.

Round Island is represented twice: once in the Ste. Anne Marine National Park, as a tiny, green, low-lying island; and once to the southeast of Praslin, as a bizarre granite tower. What they have in common is excellent snorkelling all around. The Round Island just off Victoria has a small Creole restaurant, a palm-thatched, open affair, where participants of organized tours are served a typical Seychellois menu - noon or night. (See also "Out and About in the Seychelles", p.130).

Sainte Anne Island is the largest island in the marine park just off Victoria that goes by the same name. It is dominated by the 250-metre (820-foot) Mount Ste. Anne. Unfortunately, since the government has reserved the island for its "National Youth Service", it is not open for tourism. Of historical interest is the fact that Sainte Anne was one of Lazare Picault's first discoveries (1742) and the site of one of the first white settlements (in 1770, but abandoned soon after).

Silhouette Island, third largest of the granite isles, lies 20 km (12 miles) northwest of Mahé. Its imposing silhouette is a well-known sight to those who watch the sunset at Beau Vallon. Lesser known are the riches this island has to offer to nature lovers, hikers and vacationers. For instance, in 1983 a forest was discovered in the highlands between Mt. Pot á Eau (620 metres/ 2,034 feet) and Mt. Dauban (750 metres/ 2,460 feet), the highest elevations on the island. Astonishingly, huge heretofore unknown trees were found to grow here. Other rare trees, shrubs and blossoms have persevered due to Silhouettes' isolated location and can be observed along the two trails between La Passe in the east and Grand Barbe in the west.

About 250 people inhabit the coastal area, where they practise agriculture: coconuts, cinnamon, sugar cane, tropical fruit and vegetables. One can still visit a sugar mill and an oil press, as well as a colonial-style plantation house made of wood. There are no streets at all on the island, only trails and paths. The beaches and reefs, which have only small openings for boats to enter, are ideal for snorkelling.

Because it takes two hours to get there by boat from Mahé, visitors have been rather scarce. However, travel conditions have now improved markedly. It would really be worthwhile to spend a few days, or even an entire vacation, on Silhouette, especially since the opening of the Silhouette Island Lodge in 1986. Reservations can be made with your travel agent.

Thérèse Island, located off Mahé's western coast, is a small granite isle with an elevation of 164 metres (538 feet) and a beach that is ideal for snorkelling. From the elevation - or from the boat, if you are taking part in an excursion from Mahé - you can see the great steps of Pointe l'Escalier. It is still unclear whether they are a product of nature or ceremonial structures made by the Indonesians who began to settle Madagascar in 300 A.D.

In 1987 the Seychelles Sheraton opened up its sports centre on Thérèse.

Now there is a regular ferry service free for guests - to what has become known as "Sheraton Island".

Outer Islands

To begin this section we must look at an island which has been on the Seychelles' tourist programme since April 1988 and which has already proved itself a most valuable addition.

Desroches, largest island of the Amirantes group, forms part of a huge sunken atoll, the highest elevation of which only rises a few metres above sea level. It extends for almost 10 km (6 miles) in length and is just 1 km (a little over $^1/_2$ mile) in width. The palms that grow on it are said to produce the best copra of the Indian Ocean. This makes Desroches the most important of the Amirantes islands in terms of economics, a fact that has been accentuated by its increasing popularity as a vacation site where all kinds of sports activities can be practised, including scuba diving and deep-sea fishing. One word aptly describes the backdrop provided by the flora and fauna, on land and underwater: magnificent.

A new airport services aircraft coming from Mahé, approximately 210 km (130 miles) away, and guests will find accommodation at a newly-constructed lodge.

The approximately 60 coral isles making up the Outer Islands lie to the southwest of the main archipelago, scattered over a distance of 1,000 km (over 600 miles) in the Indian Ocean - some are much closer to Africa and Madagascar than Mahé. No more than

400 people live on them, or less than 1% of the total population. Though the figures are correct, they are still misleading because most of these islands are not inhabited. Many are just atolls that have formed shallow lagoons and are hardly visible on the horizon. The islands that are arable enough to sustain a permanent settlement can actually be counted with the fingers of both hands. Otherwise, there are only a few that are either temporarily or permanently inhabited for the purposes of scientific research.

With the exception of Cöetivy, the only island lying due south of Mahé and not accessible to visitors, the Outer Islands basically form three distinct groups: the Amirantes, Farquhar and Aldabra archipelagos.

The Amirantes are situated much closer to Mahé than the other islands, being about 210-340 km (130-211 miles) away. Only Alphonse, D'Arros, Desroches, Marie Louise and Poivre are inhabited, and only half of these have a landing strip: Desroches, Marie Louise and D'Arros. Most of the islands are serviced in three-month intervals by the ship "Cinq Juin"; travellers on business have priorities here (labourers, civil servants, etc.).

Other than Desroches, which has been described previously, it is **Desnoeufs** that is especially worthy of mention. Hundreds of thousands of terns come here to brood between April and September.

The first humans to visit the Amirantes were probably Arabs in the 9th century. But it was Vasco da Gama who,

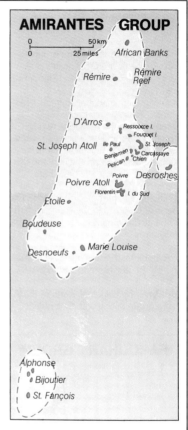

in 1502 and in the course of his second voyage to India, gave the archipelago its present name: Ilhas do Almirante (The Admiral's Islands).

Farquhar was also discovered by a Portuguese seafarer: in this instance in 1504 by João Nova. The islands that make up this group - Farquhar, Cerf, St. Pierre and Providence - lie between

720 and 820 km (447-510 miles) from Mahé.

The Farquhar islands are grouped around one of the most beautiful lagoons of the Indian Ocean. Skippers hold the atoll in esteem because it is possible to drop anchor there all year round. "Twenty-Five-Franc-Beach" is noted for its perfect beauty: two kilometres long and with powdery white sand, it drops gently into a warm turquoise sea. Copra production and fishing form the economic basis here; numerous palms and casuarinas lend an additional charm to the islands. The island of Goëlette in the southern part of the atoll is a paradise for birds, especially terns.

A landing strip was built a few years ago on the northernmost island.

Aldabra, the principal island of the Aldabra group (along with Cosmoledo, Assumption and Astove), has attracted more attention than just about any other island in the entire Seychelles archipelago. This was particularly true during the late 60's, when there was vehement resistance to a plan to use the island militarily, which would certainly have spelled the doom of this atoll and the giant tortoises living on it. But, due to international support from politicians and scientists, this fate was averted by 1967. The island was declared a nature reserve under the administration of the "Seychelles Island Foundation" (SIF), patronized by President Albert René. Since the establishment of a research station on Picard (West), Aldabra has been completely taken under the wings of science (see "Aldabra, Galapagos of the Indian Ocean" p.58).

The Cosmoledo atoll and its island Astove are about 1,050 km (650 miles) away from Mahé; Aldabra and Assumption about 1,200 km (745 miles). On the other hand, Aldabra is only 650 km (404 miles) away from the Tanzanian coast and a mere 400 km (250 miles) from Madagascar.

The Aldabra atoll was probably discovered by Arabs in the tenth century. They called it "Al-khadra" (the green one); the Portuguese turned this into "Al Hadara" and it wasn't long until Aldabra came about.

Cosmoledo has a geological background similar to Aldabra. A great number of seabirds (for example, boobies) thrive here. Many sea turtles live in the surrounding waters.

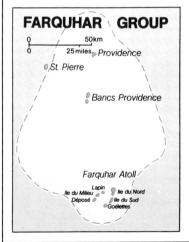

FARQUHAR GROUP

0   50km
0   25 miles   Providence

St. Pierre

Bancs Providence

Farquhar Atoll

Lapin
Ile du Milieu   Ile du Nord
Déposé   Ile du Sud
                  Goëlettes

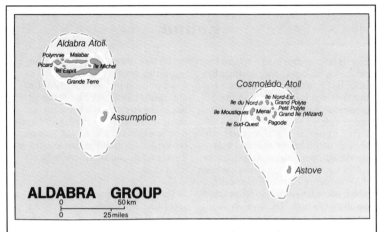

Assumption was once an important bird island. But the birds chose to brood on some of the other islands instead, meaning the process could begin whereby the bird droppings that had collected over millenia could be commercially exploited: guano has been gathered here since about 1840, amounting to approximately one million tons so far. Guano was - and continues to be - an important factor in Seychelles' exports. Traditionally, it was always sent to Mauritius, where it was used extensively in the sugar cane fields.

As there are only airstrips in Farquhar and on Astove (Aldabra Group), people and merchandise are primarily transported by boat, just as in the Amirantes. The "Cinq Juin" sails from Mahé to the principal islands of the two southern groups at regular intervals of two to three months. It is also possible to charter schooners for the trip (see "Useful Information").

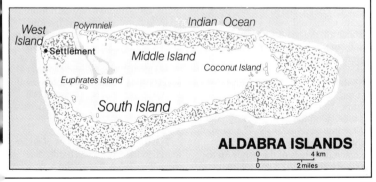

Fauna

Islands have always held a special fascination for biologists and, whether the latter be professionals or amateur enthusiasts, the fascination is always greatest in the case of islands which are as isolated as the Seychelles. For then it's possible to witness plants and animals which have developed independently over millenia. Often, the result of such isolated evolution has been the emergence of individual species which allow for extremely informative comparisons with "relatives" in their original habitat. Since the crossing of water presents an insurmountable (or, at best, a sizeable) obstacle for many species of plant and animal, their presence on an island can often be seen as evidence of the existence of a land bridge which, at some point in the course of history, linked the island with the nearest landmass. Their absence would then indicate the contrary.

Mammals

As a general rule, mammals play a subordinate role – if any role at all – in the fauna of so-called oceanic islands (i.e. islands not located in the vicinity of a continental landmass). For mammals above all, the sea does indeed represent an insurmountable divide. Apart from those brought to the islands by man (from rats and mice to cats, dogs, goats and horses), there is only one group of mammals on the Seychelles: **bats**. Their most common representative on the islands is a fruit bat, *Pteropus seychellensis*. The head of this large bat resembles that of a canine (fruit bats of the genus Pteropus are also called flying foxes). Feeding on fruit, these bats are essentially nocturnal, emerging after nightfall to forage among fruit trees – when they are usually taken for birds. Those who would like to see a fruit bat close up might go along to the Boutique Macouti in Beau Vallon, Mahé. The animals are kept there in the garden in front of the boutique; conditions are sadly far from ideal.

The *"sousouri banane" (Coleura seychellensis)* is a rare insectivorous bat found on the Seychelles; it emerges at dusk to set off on its search for nourishment. The local name of this bat clearly indicates the strong influence of French upon the Creole of the Seychelles (Fr. *chauve-souris* = bat).

Reptiles

As with mammals, most reptiles are not in a position to cross any sizeable expanse of water. Exceptions here would, of course, include reptiles such as marine turtles which have adapted to aquatic conditions (even land-living chelonians are good natural swimmers). Small reptiles rely on flotsam or boats to transport them across any larger watery divide. As far as the Seychelles are concerned, one does find skinks, geckos, chameleons and smaller snakes (all either as indigenous species or as "immigrants"), but there are no larger snakes (a fact that will doubtless reassure many a prospective visitor).

The three (harmless) types of adder found on the islands will hardly ever show their faces. Not so the agile

Day gecko

gecko. The bronze gecko *(Aeluronyx seychellensis)* likes to hunt insects on the ceilings and walls of houses and bungalows (on the smaller islands to a greater extent than on Mahé). In so doing the gecko makes a valuable contribution to visitors' comfort and helps to ensure nights of undisturbed slumber. The bright green day gecko *(Phelsuma astriata)* is usually found on trees and bushes – for example, on banana trees. It plays an important part in the fertilization of the coco-de-mer.

On those islands where there are no rats you may well encounter two endemic **skinks**: the Seychelles mabuya *(Mabuya seychellensis)* and the Wright's mabuya *(Mabuya wrightii)*. Both are harmless but do represent a threat to sea birds since they are fond of stealing the latter's eggs.

The granite islands of the Seychelles were once the habitat of larger reptiles, principally caimans, crocodiles and chelonians (tortoises and turtles). Of these original inhabitants, only the tortoises remain. That they should have survived man's merciless hunting is something of a miracle in itself: even before the Seychelles were settled, passing sailors took advantage of the numerous **giant tortoises** *(Testudo gigantea)* found on the islands to ensure a constant supply of fresh meat. Then came the first settlers: they were quick to recognize this most lucrative resource and in the space of just five years, between 1784 and 1789, a devastating 13,000 giant tortoises were sold to ship's crews taking on supplies in Mahé. Placed on their backs for the purposes of transportation, the hapless tortoises were often subjected to weeks at sea before being slaughtered and eaten.

The islanders, unwilling to forego this agreeable alternative to fish protein, followed the example of the seafarers. Since tortoises do not reproduce prolifically (sexual maturity is only reached, for example, in the twentieth year of the animal's life), the species soon faced extinction.

Nowadays we find only a few isolated examples of those original Seychelles tortoises (if, indeed, any survive at all). It is widely assumed that one or two splendid tortoises belong to their number. There's George on Cousin Island (he's taken to be a centenarian) and Agamemnon and Esmeralda on Bird Island. The name Esmeralda turned out to be an unhappy choice: it was later discovered that "she" was in fact a male. Be that as it may, Esmeralda is thought to be the oldest, largest and heaviest land tortoise in the world. At the grand old age of 150 years, Esmeralda's carapace was the subject of scientists' interest and was established to be an impressive 1.59 m (5.2 ft.) in length; s/he weighed in at 213 kilos (1989)!

Other giant tortoises you encounter on the Seychelles will more than likely have been brought there from the Aldabras. Once found on many of the islands of the Indian Ocean, giant tortoises of the species *Testudo gigantea* are now limited to the Aldabra group. Together with the Galápagos Islands (home to the species *Testudo elephantopus*). The Aldabras constitute a last refuge of giant tortoises living in their natural wild state.

At the turn of the century, the tortoise population on the Aldabras had dropped to a few thousand; decisive and rigourous protection measures were, however, sufficient to save the species from extinction and by 1988 the population had recovered to some 150,000 (see also "Aldabra, Galápagos of the Indian Ocean", p.58).

Fairly sizeable groups of tortoises now live in a partly domesticated state on Frégate, Moyenne and Denis Island. A few hundred animals have been established on Curieuse for the purposes of breeding; smaller groups live in enclosures in the Botanical Gar-

den on Mahé and in L'Union (La Digue); some hotels will even have a single tortoise on their grounds.

Although the marine turtles found in the Seychelles also belong to the class of reptiles, they are not dealt with in this chapter; see instead "Fascinating Underwater World", p.98.

Land Birds

Of all living things, birds have least difficulty gaining access to remote oceanic islands (that is, if we exclude insects and plant seeds and spores, which are carried by the wind and air currents).

The fact that of the twenty-three species of land bird found on the Seychelles seventeen are endemic (i.e. found only here) supports the theory that the islands were separated from other land masses at an early point in time. It's interesting to note here that the endemic land birds of the Seychelles do in fact have "distant relatives" in other parts of the world. They are therefore not as individual and unique as, say, the (extinct) dodo of Mauritius. Be that as it may, the land birds of the Seychelles will prove a treasure-trove for both professional and hobby ornithologists ... and for anyone who takes pleasure in the wondrous creations of Nature.

Distribution of most species is limited to two or three islands (mostly outside Mahé), which means that those interested in tracking down and observing birds in their natural habitat will need to devote time and effort to the undertaking. To have a fair chance of success one should estimate around

14 days (includes visits to islands which are also home to a wealth of sea birds, islands such as Cousin and Aride).

It is not the place of a travel guide to give detailed and comprehensive information about distinguishing features, habitat and habits of the various birds. Such a task rightly remains the preserve of specialist literature. Still, a brief survey at this point may well be of assistance in highlighting those endemic species and subspecies which one does have a good chance of encountering. Details are given of locations where sightings are most likely to occur.

Black Parrot
(Coracopsis nigra barklyi)
In the Vallée de Mai National Park on Praslin, on or near fruit bearing trees of all kinds.

Magpie Robin
(Copsychus sechellarum)
Distribution worldwide limited to around 40 specimens on Frégate. Although the magpie robin is now so rare, it can in fact often be seen near the settlement on Frégate. If you have flown to the island for a day's visit, be sure to make at least a cursory tour straight away since as the sun rises these birds become a rarer sight.

Black Paradise Flycatcher
(Terpsiphone corvina)
Known locally as the veuve (= widow), found on La Digue in the specially created La Digue Veuve Reserve.

Brush Warbler
(Calamocichla sechellensis)
Cousin Island is the only place in the world where this rare bird breeds; there are around 300 specimens on the island.

Turtle Dove
(Streptopelia picturata rostrata)
The original phenotype (rust-coloured head) is now only found on Cousin and Cousine; otherwise the dove has to a great extent interbred with the Madagascar turtle dove (grey head).

Seychelles Blue Pigeon
(Alectroenas pulcherrima)
A particularly colourful pigeon; found on higher ground on Mahé, the plateau of Frégate and in the Vallée de Mai on Praslin.

Seychelles Sunbird
(Nectarinia dussumieri)
Found on practically all the larger islands, on flowering trees and shrubs of all kinds.

Seychelles Kestrel
(Falco araea)
On Mahé, seen perched on buildings and telephone masts.

Seychelles Fody
(Foudia sechellarum)
The locals call the fody "toc toc"; found on Cousine, Frégate and most frequently on Cousin.

Seychelles Grey White-Eye
(Zosterops modesta)
Found in the highlands of Mahé.

Seychelles Bulbul
(Hypsipetes crassirostris)
In upland wooded areas of all the granite islands.

Seychelles Cave Swiftlet
(Collocalia francica elaphra)
Can be seen in flight on all the granite islands; the swiftlet nests in the granite cliffs of the islands.

Seychelles Bare-Legged Scops Owl
(Otus insularis)
Lives in the wooded highlands of Mahé.

Seychelles Moorhen
(Gallinula chloropus sechellarum)
An endemic subspecies of the moorhen, a species widely distributed throughout the world. Found primarily on Aride and Cousin, usually near freshwater pools but also at considerable distances from the latter.

Cattle Egret
(Bubulcus ibis)
A frequent and fond visitor of fish markets (including that of Victoria), taking the place, one might say, of the seagulls which are not found on the Seychelles.

Of the birds which arrived on the Seychelles with the settlers, three are particularly conspicuous:

Barred Ground Dove
(Geopelia striata)
These small, very tame doves have long since ceased to be afraid of man. If you're enjoying a meal alfresco you're almost sure to find them hopping about at your feet.

Madagascar Fody
(Foudia madagascariensis)
Also known as (in Creole) as the serin or cardinal, the Madagascar fody is the most conspicuous bird on the islands – true at least during the breeding season when the male's plumage turns a brilliant scarlet (normally it is greyish brown like that of the female).

Indian Mynah
(Acridotheres tristis)
A "noisy" bird, the shrill call of which can be heard on all the islands except Cousin and Aride.

Madagascar Fody

Sea Birds

The Seychelles represent one of the most important habitats and "bases" for sea birds in the whole of the Indian Ocean. The shallow waters of the Mahé plateau provide a wealth of food and on the virtually uninhabited islands of Bird, Aride and Cousin neither man nor natural predators pose a threat to birdlife. In addition, strict protection measures are now enforced in the Seychelles. Instigated in cooperation with international organizations such as the British Royal Society, these apply in particular to those islands outside the Mahé plateau which are the chosen habitat of sea birds. This is the case on the African Banks and Desnoeufs (Amirantes), Goëiette (Farquhar group), and Aldabra and Cosmoledo

(Aldabra group). Thanks to the isolation of these islands, the world of the sea birds living there has survived almost untouched. Due to the lack of flight connections and accommodation it is unlikely that such islands will be included on a "normal" tourist itinerary. Since wildlife and environmental protection are the order of the day here, it is hardly surprising that this should be so. Those with a special interest in such areas (i.e. ornithologists or divers) should have the opportunity to charter a schooner in Victoria or on La Digue.

Compared with such isolated islands, it is relatively easy to gain access to Bird, Aride and Cousin. For details of plane and boat connections, see the chapter "Out and About in the Seychelles", p.130.

Among the sea birds of the Seychelles, the **terns** (or **sea swallows**) are the most widely distributed.

Of them, the **sooty tern** *(Sterna fuscata)* enjoys special status in a number of respects. For one thing, it cannot be considered entirely indigenous since it is only between April or May and October or November that the sooty terns search out their traditional breeding places on the islands. Whence they come and where they spend the rest of the year remains one of ornithology's great mysteries. It has even been suggested that the birds are capable of sustaining flight for months, gliding gracefully above the surface of the water.

The second special claim to fame of the sooty terns is that, as far as numbers are concerned, they represent the largest single group of birds to be found on the islands. The flocks which constitute the largest breeding colonies on the Islands of Desnoeufs, Bird and

Aride amount to millions! Their nests – for the most part a barely noticeable hollow in the ground, and only ever containing one egg – completely cover extensive areas of sand. Some 35,000 breeding pairs have been counted on just one hectare.

The following is a survey of the most important sea birds to be found in the Seychelles.

Fairy Tern
(Gygis alba monte)
The most graceful of the terns, white with a blue beak and black eyes. A characteristic of the fairy tern is that it lays a single egg, not in a nest but in the fork of a tree or even on bare rocks. Found on almost all the islands, numbers of fairy terns began to drop steadily (particularly on Mahé) after the arrival of the African barn owl (Tyto alba affinis). This bird of prey had been "imported" by planters at the beginning of the 1950s in order to keep down the rat population. Since the barn owl has been declared fair game for hunters, numbers of fairy terns have increased markedly.

Roseate Tern
(Sterna dougallii arideensis)
The most colourful tern; the feet are red and the beak red and black. As the Latin name reveals, this is a special subspecies, the largest colony of which worldwide is to be found on Aride; there is a smaller colony on Bird Island.

Lesser or Black Noddy
(Anous tenuirostris)
Builds nests of leaves and seaweed in casuarinas and other trees. This tern is found primarily on Aride and Cousin; the largest colony in the world is on

92

Aride. The name "noddy" refers to the bird's habit of nodding its head during courtship displays.

Common or Brown Noddy
(Anous stolidus pileatus)
Brown plumage, is larger than the lesser or black noddy; more powerful wing movements in flight; nests in palms or on cliffs. The common or brown noddy is encountered on almost all the Seychelles islands; the largest colonies are on Aride and Cousin.

Bridled Tern
(Sterna anaethetus)
One of the less numerous and more timid terns of the Seychelles; predominantly on Aride and Cousin. Can often be seen perched in casuarinas but nests on the ground – either amid scanty vegetation or under a rock overhang.

Great Frigate Bird
(Fregata minor)
and Lesser Frigate Bird
(Fregata ariel)
With a wing span of up to 2 m (6 $\frac{1}{2}$ ft.), the frigate birds are acrobatic and swift in flight. They feed on flying fish or on fish, either plucking them from the surface of the water themselves or siezing them from other sea birds with an aggression which has earned them the name "man-of-war bird". Can be

seen gliding over the smaller granite islands, sometimes over Denis Island, too. Land to rest on Aride and Cousin, breed on Aldabra.

White-Tailed Tropic Bird
(Phaethon lepturus)
Can be seen on Bird, Cousin and Aride (largest colony) as well as in higher-lying areas of Mahé. Flies great distances over the open sea, feeding by swooping on fish. Breeds in sheltered spots on the ground or in trees.

Red-Talled Tropic Bird
(Phaethon rubricauda)
The rarest sea bird of the Seychelles; Aride is the only granite isle upon which it can be seen. Appears somewhat more frequently on Aldabra and Cosmoledo.

Wedge-Tailed Shearwater
(Thyellodroma pacifica chlororhyncha)
Found mainly on Cousin and Aride; breeds between October and March in caves in the granite cliffs; mainly nocturnal in its habits.

Little Shearwater
(Puffinus assimilis nicolae)
Similar to the wedge-tailed shearwater in both distribution and habits; the little shearwaters are less common, however, and, as the name suggests, smaller.

There are a great many species of migratory birds which can be encountered on the Seychelles on a seasonal basis. To name just a few: curlew sandpipers, grey or black-bellied plovers, whimbrels, ruddy turnstones and sanderlings. On Aldabra, herons and flamingos can also be seen.

1. *White-tailed Tropic Bird*
2. *Great Frigatebird*
3. *Black Paradise Flycatcher*
4. *Common Noddy*
5. *Sooty Tern*

Flora

The vegetation of the Seychelles is such as will delight and enthral from the very first moment of one's arrival in Mahé. The epitome of lush tropical vegetation: palms with slender fronds or outstretched fans; shrubs blossoming in a riot of colour; spreading trees, their dark green leaves smooth and polished, some heavy with decidedly foreign-looking fruits. The effect is unmistakeably exotic...which is just what it should be: vegetation typical of a land at this latitude.

Nevertheless, our enthusiasm shouldn't blind us to the fact that we are looking here at the second generation of Seychelles vegetation. The first generation, the product of several hundred million years evolution, was "removed" by man within the space of just two hundred years. Gigantic trees must once have covered the islands (and in particular the granite islands), their dense canopy of tropical primeval foliage extending from the coast to the heights. The first settlers spoke with wonderment of these trees...and then proceeded promptly to fell them for ship and house building. There apparently wasn't even time for chroniclers to record accurate details for posterity.

Today there are still isolated areas where it is possible to gain an impression of the structure and luxuriance of the primeval forests which so enthralled those first settlers. This is the case in the higher, less accessible regions of Mahé, on Silhouette, and in the Vallée de Mai on Praslin, the latter a celebrated example of the palm forests of the Seychelles.

Some endemic, inherently Seychellois plants have, of course, survived the course of time. But these are as nothing compared with the many species which have been imported or transmitted to the islands at some point and are now indigenous. These constitute the new, second generation of plants.

It has, however, been possible to establish the existence of 75 endemic plants, i.e. plants which are found here and nowhere else in the world in a natural state. It would be wholly unrealistic to attempt to list them all – let alone describe them – within the framework of a travel guide. That rightly remains the sphere of a comprehensive and authoritative work, one which deserves to be mentioned here: Francis Friedmann's *Flowers and Trees of the Seychelles*, 1986, only available in the Seychelles (see also the list of recommended literature in the Useful information section). Still, a brief summary of the extremely varied and fascinating flora of the Seychelles would certainly not be amiss. Such a survey should definitely include those endemic species which you may well, or indeed are certain to, encounter along the way. Perhaps it will inspire you to search out the plants systematically – something which is more than worthwhile!

As far as endemic species are concerned, the showpiece of the Seychelles is the **coco-de-mer** *(Lodoicea maldivica)*. In the plant world this impressive species of palm must surely rank beside the biblical cedar of Lebanon and the mighty giant sequoia of

California. The last home of the coco-de-mer is in the Vallée de Mai National Park on Praslin.(See also the entries under "Highlights" p.41, and "Coco-de-Mer, the fruit that came from the sea", p.55) It is in the Vallée de Mai Park above all that one also finds the five species of palm and the three species of vacoa (screwpine) which are endemic to the Seychelles.

The Morne Seychellois National Park on Mahé is particularly rich in endemic species. Which is not to say that one stumbles upon such every step of the way. They are now in fact limited to areas where difficulties of access afford them some protection, having "withdrawn" there in the course of time to escape the encroachments of civilization. Taking part in organized walks (with a guide) through these areas is a good way of glimpsing the wonders of such remote regions of the islands (see the section on hiking in "Sports in the Seychelles", p.141).

As examples of remarkable endemic species to be found at higher altitudes on Mahé, we might single out a tree and a climbing plant. The **bois méduse** or **jellyfish tree**, as a rule only 6-8 m (20-26 ft.) high and a distant relative of the camelia, differs so markedly from other plants that the botanical family *Medusagynacae* was created for it. The tree owes its common name to its capsulate fruits, which look like tiny jellyfishes and liberate winged seeds. The **pitcher plant** *(Nepenthes pervillei)*, an insectivorous creeping plant, spreads out over areas of granite rock. The leaves of the plant have adapted to form pitcher-like organs which attract and trap insects. The pitcher plant grows not only on Mahé (on Mt. Coton and Mt. Jasmin) but

also, among other places, on Mt. Pot-à-Eau on Silhouette.

Silhouette also boast one of the rarest trees of the Seychelles, the **bosquea** *(Trilepisium madagascariense)*; and as recently as 1983 a new tree and a new type of forest were discovered there – the **mapou de grand bois**.

To close the round of botanical sensations, the most beautiful flowering shrub of the Seychelles, the **bois citron** or **Writh's gardenia** *(Rothmania annae)*, is found nowhere else in the world but on the island of Aride.

Bois Méduse or Jellyfish Tree – in blossom and bearing fruit

As part of a general Suvey of Seychelles flora, it is interesting to note how indigenous an endemic species exist side by side with plants which were introduced by man – and in particular with those which are now cultivated commercially. A brief outline should sufice here to throw some light upon the matter for both amateur enthusiasts and those with more knowledge in the field. As is usual when considering the vegetation of tropical regions, the various vegetational zones will be defined according to altitude.

The **lower vegetational zone** comprises coastal and lowland vegetation and includes in the first instance **mangrove flats**. Nowadays there are only isolated examples of the latter: for instance, on Mahé at Anse Boileau and between Port Glaud and Port Launay, on Silhouette at Grand Barbe, and to a larger extent on Aldabra. Of the eight kinds of mangrove found on the Seychelles (where they are known as *manglier*), it is the widely-distributed **manglier Hauban** *(Rhizophora mucronata)* with its arched stilt roots which is most conspicuous. The fruits of the **manglier pomme** *(Xylocarpus granatum)* ar roughly the size of grapefruits and contain many-sided seeds. Once the fruit has been opened, it demands inordinate patience to return the seeds to their natural state, which would explain why the popular name of the manglier pomme is *"manglier patience"* of "Chinese puzzle".

The soil composition of the lowlands which border on the coast is determined by sands washed ashore by flood tides and deposits swept down from the mountains. Known to the Seychellois as "plateaux", these lowlands reach a height of some 300 m (984 ft.) and were once the site of extensive coastal forests. The latter have long since disappeared almost entirely in the wake of settlement an the extensive cultivation of specific crops. Of these, the **coconut palm** *(Cocos nucifera)* remains the most widespread. Present on the islands when the first arrivals landed, today's cultivated palms are the products of careful selection aimed at a maximum copra yield.

Following the coconut, the most common tree is the **takamaka** *(Calophyllum inophyllum)*. It is the wide, shady crown of takamakas that afford such pleasant relief from the heat of the sun on the beaches of Beau Vallon and Grand Anse (both Mahé) and at Anse la Passe on Silhouette.

There are a number of smaller and medium-sized trees which also flourish along the coastal strip. The **var** *(Hibiscus tiliaceus)* has large yellow blossoms with purple centres and is quite outstanding. In addition, there is the **bois de table** *(Heritiera littoralis)* and the **gayac** *(Intsia bijuga)*. The hard wood of both trees rendered them invaluable to the shipbuilders of bygone years; the gayac is now quite a rare sight.

The **sandragon** *(Pterocarpus indicus)* and the **banyan** *(Ficus benghalensis)* can both grow to be veritable giants. The numerous aerial roots of the banyan make it particularly conspicuous; a splendid specimen can be admired in front of Plantation House of Frégate.

For reafforestation programmes, fast-growing, and in some instances foreign, species wre employed: the **albizzia** *(Albizzia falcatal)*, for examle, the slenderest and tallest tree on the

Seychelles (up to 30 m/over 98 ft. in height!); **santol** *(Sandoricum indicum)*; **casuarina** *(Casuarina equisetifolia)*, the latter a familiar sight lining beach and boulevard but also a valuable component of reafforestation schemes aimed at stemming erosion in the hills.

The **central and lower vegetational zones** cadn be said to overlap in so far as the many plants which constitute the typical vegetation of the central zone are also found on the cliffs and rocky slopes of the "plateaux". It ist here, for example, that we find the various palms – among others, the aforementioned coco-de-mer. Then there ist the multitude of fairly common trees and shrubs: **bois de natte** *(Mimosops sechellarum)*; **bois cuillère** *(Tabernaemontana coffeoides)*, so named because the open fruits of the tree resemble spoons; **bois de lait** *(Euphorbia pyrifolia)*, which can take hold in the narrowest of clefts in the rocks and often serves as "host" to the **wild vanilla**. A number of different types of **orchid** also thrive at this altitude, particularly at home in the shady undergrowth. Of these, the **tropic bird orchid** *(Angraecum eburneum brongniartianum)* is probably the most beautiful.

The **upper vegetational zone** comprises land lying 600 m and more (almost 2,000 ft.) above se level – found only on Mahé and Silhouette. At this altitude cloud forests prevail, yearly precipitation amounts to 2 500 mm (98 ins.) and more, and atmospheric humidity is high. Primeval forests comprising substantial stands of **capucin** *(Northea hornei)* but also **manglier de grand bois** *(Glionetia sericea)* and **bois rouge** *(Dillenia ferruginea)* spread up to summit regions (on Mahé, 900 m/over 2,900 ft. above sea level). **Vacoas** (marron, de Revière) and **lataniers** (feuille, Hauban) also grow at these heights. Trees which stand between 5 m (16 ft.) and 15 m (50 ft.) in height, beneath them the undergrowth: a lavish profusion of shrubs and ferns, mosses and orchids... there are 80 species of fern alone!

Even if most of the names don't mean a great deal to the nonspecialist, the abundance of lush green leaves and the magnificence of brightly-coloured blossoms are there for one and all to enjoy. They will mark every day of your stay on the Seychelles, regardless of the time of year you choose for your trip.

As far as **commercial cultivation** is concerned, visitors enjoy the fruits of Seychellois labours quite literally – in the shape of succulent fruits at the breakfast buffet and delicious desserts after dinner. Every item on offer looks as good as it tastes, which is why fruits and vegetables are dealt with in a separate chapter, "Bon Appetit à la Seychelloise", see p.110.

Of those plants which are of commercial importance to the islands, the **coconut** has already been mentioned as heading the list. As far as export statistics are concerned, it is **cinnamon** *(Cinnamomum zeylanicum)* which follows on the heels of copra. The leaves of the cinnamon tree (the bark of which provides the valued spice) are red at first but turn bright green in the later stages of growth. **Tea** also plays an increasingly important role in exports. For more details on both cinnamon and tea, see "Economic Aspects", p.101.

A final word: those who are interested in the whole (wide) botanical spectrum of the Seychelles – in very general terms – should definitely make a point of visiting the botanical garden in Victoria. The garden provides an excellent overall impression of the flora of the Seychelles and, besides a number of smaller specimens of coco-demer palms and an enclosure for giant tortoises, contains a beautiful orchid garden with some 150 species.

Fascinating Underwater World

An incredible variety of colourful tropical life thrives in the waters around the Seychelles. The coral reefs, more than anything else, provide an ideal and protected habitat for marine fauna. Some 200 different species of fish alone – of a total of 900 found in the waters of the Seychelles – have been registered in the reefs of the Granite Islands. In order to protect this sensitive submarine biotope, the government of the Seychelles has enforced stiff regulations. For instance, several marine national parks have been established, the best known of which is the Ste. Anne Marine National Park. Is lies just before Victoria and thus makes it relatively easy for one to experience this underwater world. Spearfishing has been strictly prohibited and the collecting of shells in the water or on the beach is forbidden in designated areas (marked by "Shelling prohibited" notices). In the same spirit, the government did not hesitate to declare certain marine areas off limits to divers when it was discovered that damage had been purposefully perpetrated there, as in the case not that long ago of Anse Cocos.

All of this has meant that the coral banks and their flora and fauna are in a remarkably healthy state, quite in contrast to the plundered reefs found in other parts of the world. The fish here are not afraid of humans; on the contrary, they are so tame they can be hand fed.

Such a memorable experience will problably be limited to scuba divers, who can stay under water long enough to "befriend" the fish. But even if you just snorkel along directly beneath the surface, the fish will behave as if you simply didn't exist. Thus you can easily observe the teeming, colourful life between brain, branch and table corals. Of the approximately 2 500 species of coral found in the world, more than 100 abound in the waters of the Seychelles. Red, blue, white and black, they form the perfect background for the fantastic colours of the fish, such as the coral-eating parrotfish in hues that range from orange to cobalt blue, the reddish-brown turkeyfish (whose poisonous spiny dorsal fin should be watched out for), or the yellow-black-white butterflyfish which uses its long and pointed snout to search for prey in the tiniest nooks and crannies of the reef.

Even if names like clownfish, angelfish, zebra lionfish or trumpetfish don't mean much to you, it is still a pleasure to observe them in their natural, unspoilt environment (for tips on underwater photography see "Photo Tips" p.150).

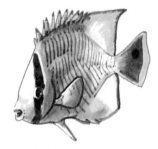

Butterflyfish

The reef, however, is not the only marine environment in the Seychelles that is worthy of note. Two additional ones lie just beyond the reef. One is found in the shallow waters of the large underwater plateau upon which the granite islands of the Mahé and Praslin group stand. Here, in clear water with a visibility of up to 50 metres (165 feet), live the somewhat larger species like batfish, surgeonfish, grunts and spotted morays (see chapter "A Paradise for Suba Divers and Snorkellers" p.52). The third environment is found along the edge of the plateau, just off the islands of Bird and Denis, where the sea bed quickly drops down to a depth of 1,800 metres (5,905 feet). This is the playground of tuna, sharks, barracudas, wahoos, sailfish and marlin, some of which are prize catches for deep-sea fishermen.

All three marine environments abound in molluscs. Among the 300 or more species found in the Seychelles, the most prominent are cowries and toxiglossids. The former have glossy, porcelain-like shells that come in light or dark colours and are often spotted. Some of the latter have a poisonous proboscis (a dartlike projection) that can even be dangerous to man. Conchs and tritons are masterly creations of nature and a true wonder to behold.

But coral, fish and molluscs are not all that the Seychelles marine world has to offer. The marine turtles still have to be mentioned, the four largest species of which are represented here: hawksbill *(Eretmochelys imbricata)*, common loggerhead *(Caretta caretta)*, leatherback *(Dermochelys coriacea)* and green turtle *(Chelonia mydas)*. Whereas the first two species are regularly found along the shores of certain islands, the latter two tend to move about in the waters around the Seychelles, especially off Aldabra and Cosmoledo (they have become rare in the area of the granite islands). This is undoubtedly due to the fact that the green turtle has been hunted massively over the centuries for its tasty meat. Today it has been placed under strict governmental protection. Only the local inhabitants are allowed to catch a limited number of turtles (for noncommercial purposes) and a set quota is established for the entire Seychelles archipelago each year. The argument used here is that the western region of the Indian Ocean is the only place on earth where the green turtle is not endangered. Compared to the number of eggs and baby turtles that fall prey to sea birds, crabs and predacious fish, the annual catch is very low. Furthermore, male green turtles also rob eggs so that it is sensible to control their numbers by allowing only males to be included in the yearly quota.

The hawksbill and common loggerhead turtles are more widely distributed and appear in greater numbers. The hawksbill is much sought after because of its valuable shell. Tortoise shell is of economic importance to the Seychelles as it is used in the textiles industry as well as in the production of jewellery, the latter sold primarily to tourists.

Even if it is true that there are a .greater number of these turtles in the Seychelles than, for instance, in the Caribbean, it is still a fact that the species as a whole is threatened by extinction. It was therefore placed under protection according to the Washington Convention. For this reason, it is prohibited in most Western countries to import turtle shells, or souvenirs made therefrom (see also "Souvenirs", p.146).

Hawksbill
(Eretmochelys imbricata)

Green Turtle
(Chelonia mydas)

Economic Aspects

Those who spend their vacations on sunny isles like the Seychelles will hardly (or will choose not to) notice that all is not perfect in paradise, that there are also many problems and many causes for concern. This applies, for instance, to the economy.

The problem here is mainly rooted in the ambivalence of the situation. On the one hand, the Seychelles have been blessed by nature with everything that a tourist could possibly desire: rich flora and fauna, an enviable climate with warmth and ample sunshine, absolutely unique landscapes and beaches. On the other hand, the islands posses no natural resources either below or above the ground. Even the topsoil itself yields little in terms of agriculture. Only about 50 % of it is arable, and this includes the coastal regions which are dominated by coconut palms. For other agricultural endeavours like the planting of vegetables, for instance, Mahé has no more than 10 % of its total land area available; the rest is made up of mountains, forests, beaches and rocks.

This has already led to one of the major problems facing the Seychelles today: how to supply the needs of the inhabitants and visitors. Of course, in the days befor the advent of tourism, up until 1972, the sea provided sufficient fish and the plantations enough copra, spices, fruit and vegetables to maintain a smaller population than exists today. But even back then, the main staple, rice, had to be imported for lack of available farmland. At that time this was the responsibility of the British colonial administration...

With the advent of airborne tourism in the Seychelles in 1972, the situation changed rapidly. By 1976 there were already some 50,000 visitors that needed to be provided for, along with a population that hat risen by about 10 % to a total of more than 60,000. And this meant more than the bare essentials because the demand for consumer goods had attained much higher levels.

Thus there was only one possible solution: imports. Meat from Australia, butter from Singapore or Holland, cheese from France and wine from the latter or from South Africa, all for consumption by tourists. Not to mention luxury items like expensive spirits and cigarettes.

Imports that both cost and generate money.
The dilemma has remained the same: no imports, no tourists; no tourists no imports, expecially not for use by the Seychelles' own population. Whatever cash the islands generate through tourism – and this makes up about 95 % of generated earnings – flows back to foreign countries for the greater part in order to meet the needs of the selfsame tourists! No wonder, then, that the government is desperately trying to expand the basis for self-sufficiency. It has intruduced tax benefits to further agricultural production and has provided loans for fishermen to enable them to purchase more modern and efficient fishing craft. New plants for the production of cigarettes and beer are intended not only to reduce dependency on foreign imports, but also to provide additional jobs.

These and other endeavours, however, face limitations imposed by the natural environment. Three examples will illustrate the situation.

The supply of vegetables has improved markedly in recent years and, depending upon the season (= monsoon period), includes familiar products such as carrots, tomatoes, cabbages and aubergines, as well as more exotic ones like patole, squash, yam and manioc. But the apparently rich selection available at the Saturday market in Victoria cannot belie the fact that the actual growing of vegetables on the islands is problematic and the harvest hardly suffices to meet the demands.

The variety of tropical fruit available leaves little to be desired. The spectrum ranges from bananas, pineapples, passion fruits and citrus fruits to golden apples, jamalaques, mangos and papayas. Breadfruit and jackfruit usually remain the choice of the Seychellois, who prepare them as vegetables. But the fruits that are consumed between the breakfast buffet and the evening cocktail have to be imported for the greater part.

The same holds true for the milk in your coffee and the steak on your plate. Stockraising has been very limited due to lack of grazing lands. If you keep an eye out for it, you might occasionally catch a glimpse of a so-called "Creole cow", dark grey to black in colour, quite small but with a relatively large, hornless head. It is a special Seychellois cross between European an Madagascan (zebu) breeds that has adapted to the climate and food sources on the islands. Its role in the local supply of meat - rather than milk - is minor; the raising of pigs and poultry has a more prominent position here.

In all, meat, milk, fruit and vegetables comprise about half of the total food imports of the Seychelles - or three times the amount of the imported main staple, rice.

New no. 1 in exports: fish.

Fish plays a dual role in the economy: once as a traditional staple of the local population and then as an export product. In recent years fish has replaced copra as the island's main export. this is an obvious result of systematic efforts to make better use of the sheer unlimited supply of fish in the waters around the Seychelles, for example, by extending the fishing zone around each island 100 nautical miles. The goal of an ambitious projekt known as the "East Coast Project" is to establish Victoria's harbour as a centre for the tuna industry in the western Indian Ocean. An effective tuna cannery is already in operation, as well as a small packaging company, which became necessary when the exportation of fresh fish doubled from 1986 to 1987. As far as tuna is concerned, the Seychelles depend primarily on fishing fleets from France and Spain, but one also encounters trawlers under Mauritian, Japanese, Cyprian, Panamanian and Russian flags.

More than all other economic programmes, the "East Coast Project" is a manifestation of the Seychelles' efforts to expand their economic base by providing viable alternatives to the "monocultures" of tourism and copra.

As for the traditional export products, copra and spices, new factors need now be considered. Both still have a market, but, due to increased international competition, they show stagnating or sinking export tendencies rather than the other way around. Nevertheless, because of its internationally recogized quality, the copra industry in the Seychelles still finds loyal customers. Production in recent years reached 2,500 tonnes – at much lower prices, however.

Cinnamon, once second and now third mainstay of the export industry, has been severely affected by fluctuations in the world market. After having outstripped copra production in the 1960's, when Southeast Asian nations were embroiled in war and thus unable to deliver, the production of cinnamon rind dropped from 1,300 tonnes in 1973 to a mere 400 tonnes in 1981. Furthermore, decades of overexploitation, in which the large cinnamon trees were literally robbed of their bark, led to their rapid and untimely demise. That production went on at all was primarily due to mynah birds, which spread the seeds of the cinnamon trees all over the island of Mahé. Single or groups of "wild" trees thus appeared in various places. Consequently, cinnamon production in the Seychelles is no longer a plantation venture, but a matter of strenuous collecting and drying. Despite all this, production reached a new peak in 1986 with 1,200 tonnes – though coupled with severe price cuts. The periodic enterprise of distilling cinnamon oil from

Copra Is Not Just Copra

First of all, what is copra? To put it succinctly: the shredded and dried kernel of coconut. More specifically, copra is made up of 60 - 65 % fat, about 20 % carbohydrates, some 8 % raw protein and close to 4 % water. When pressed it furnishes coconut oil, which is used for the production of glycerine and forms the basic ingredient for synthetic resins. Refined, coconut oil is used as cooking fat or in the manufacture of candles, soap and shampoo.

This short definition applies to copra in general, but is says very little about the matter of quality. It is here that the Seychelles come into their own: their copra ranks among the best in the world, a fact that is acknowledged internationally by experts, scientists, chemists and consumers. The latter are primarily represented by Pakistanis. They purchase almost the entire copra harvest of the Seychelles and thus stand at the very top of the list of export customers. In 1986 alone, 2,374 tonnes of copra were exported to Pakistan.

The Pakistanis do not import shredded copra. Instead, the prefer halved nuts, or "copra cups", including the hard, fibrous shell. They do so for both culinary and religious purposes. In Islamic Pakistan religious ceremonies are conducted during which believers eat form a large communal pot. Rice and spices are scooped out of it with a copra cup which had its hard shell removed previously. The "cup" is then eaten together with its contents with great relish. This is why top quality copra is just good enough for them. And they get the best from the Seychelles — for various reasons.

Skilled workers halve the coconuts with an exact stroke the machete and then place them out to dry in the sun. They turn the halved nuts at regular intervals to guarantee uniform drying. The slightest mistake can ruin the meat or render it tasteless. Therefore it is preferable to use only ripe coconuts, which have already acquired a certain degree of dryness.

Normally, agile pickers climb up the palms and then toss down the nuts for later gathering. This is indeed a rational method of havesting, especially in the case of huge plantations in the Philippines, Malaysia or Sri Lanka. But the problem here is that only those coconuts that fall on their own have attained the right degree of ripeness. The palms in the Seychelles have the virtue of waiting for just the right moment to drop their nuts as perfect "copra cups". Much to the benefit of export figures ...

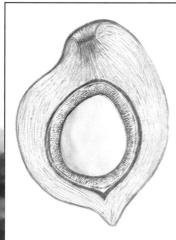

Cross section of a coconut

ly supplied by the plantation that was established in 1962 in Mahé, located along the Forêt Noir Rd., which joins Victoria with Port Glaud. As only seedlings of the finest tea plants were originally chosen, the Seychelles have become fairly successful exporters as well. Besides normal teas, there is also an excellent vanilla tea on offer. A trip to the so-called Tea Factory has become one of the popular diversions for visitors.

Efforts to strengthen the economic base in the Seychelles with other tropical products have been relegated to history. Coffee, cocoa, cardamom and cotton never stood a chance against competitors, especially the United States.

The pepper and nutmeg fiasco had origins that could be called tragic. In 1771 cinnamon, pepper and nutmeg grew splendidly in the "spice gardens" of Anse Royale. But, in 1780, unidentified ships were seen approaching the island and the overseer of the gardens, M. de Romainville, fearing a British attack and not wanting the plantation to fall into their hands, set it on fire (a popular measure in those days, as demonstrated by the Dutch in Malacca). One can well imagine the shock when it turned out that the vessels were French! Only the sturdier cinnamon trees survived the flames and thus provided the basis for future cultivation.

the leaves has presently lost its commercial significance due to synthetic products and price drops.

Vanilla, once the third-ranking plant in the Seychelles, used to play an important economic role. Around 1900, for example, annual production was 70 tonnes, at a price of 50,000 rupees per tonne. But the market broke down soon after. More recently, the production of vanilla has almost ceased entirely because a parasite has befallen the plants in Mahé and has thus far resisted all efforts to combat it.

In contrast, there has been a very positive development in a product that is relatively new to the Seychelles: tea. The local market for it is almost entire-

Expanding the infrastructure
In viewing the economic achievements of the Seychelles since independence in 1976 and, above all, since the revolution of 1977, one should not disregard the high investments made in the

sectors of health, education and transportation. Further necessary improvements in the infrastructure (also pertaining to tourism) are now underway. Among these is a more efficient road connection between Victoria and the airport. Construction on this road has already begun, which, like the international airport finished in 1971, is being built at great cost along a strip of ocean, between the shore and reef, because Mahe's coastline is too narrow for another alternative. And all this is being done despite the fact that cement is not produced locally (red granite being the only rock available). This again entails importing every sack, every tonne.

The attempts to create new possibilities and jobs in the industrial sector meet with one decisive obstacle: the absolute lack of industrially useful resources. Therefore these activities have focused around construction and ship repair, as well as skilled handiwork such as woodwork and metalwork. Nevertheless, there are many plans to develop new initiatives.

There is one more "product" – albeit one that unfortunately does not require intensive labour – that has almost unexpectedly established itself as an export hit: stamps. The tastefully designed little pieces of paper have not only called international attention to the Seychelles, but also generated much-needed foreign exchange earnings.

Tourism – Money-Spinner and Problem Child

As far as tourism is concerned, the Seychelles embody both the late developer and the high-flier...and have first-hand knowledge of the hard fall that can follow a meteoric rise to fame and fortune.

As the travel boom began to make waves in Europe at the start of the 1970s, and people decided to head for overseas destinations, the Seychelles were no more than a dot on the tourist map. It was hardly worth mentioning either the few passengers who came ashore from their cruise liners or the affluent globetrotters who moored their yachts in Victoria's harbour.

This was to change drastically in 1982 when the islands, till then only accessible via a long and inconvient sea crossing (in 16 days from Marseille, 5 from Bombay or – the most favourable option – 3 days from Mombasa in Kenya), were opened to air traffic. In anticipation, so to speak, of the Seychelles' pending independence –declared in 1976 –the British colonial powers had built an international airport, a sort of birthday present to the young republic. The airport meant that all at once the islands were easily accessible via swift, direct air links.

If 1970 had clocked up a mere 1,600 visitors by boat, 1972 saw the arrival of an amazing 15,000 by air. It was 1972, then, which marked the beginning of the Seychelles' breathtaking rise to touristic fame. In 1979 the number of visitors reached an interim high of just under 80,000, but unfortunately – to the great disappointment of all official bodies – could not be sustained at that level.

Yet everything had started out so promisingly. Showing considerable skill in improvisation, hotels had been built, roads modernised or even constructed afresh, and problems of personnel and services overcome in a quite masterly fashion. And those who came – mostly "highclass" tourists – were amazed and enchanted by the newly-discovered paradise on earth.

1980-1982: Three years of recession

Why, after such an auspicious beginning, should tourism begin to wane? This question fired many a discussion and various theories were put forward in explanation. The official Seychelles version was that an economic recession in the industrialized nations of the world had meant that target groups of tourists no longer had necessary financial means at their disposal. There was certainly some truth in this – let us say that visitors (both actual and prospective) had become increasingly sensitive to the price of a Seychelles holiday. And something which had been overlooked magnanimously in the early euphoric days of prospering enterprise and agreeable sojourns became a source of disgruntlement: namely, the (declining) standards, most noticeable in the service sector and brought about by displacement within traditional society and the ensuing social tension. Fishermen and farm workers who had abandoned their nets and laid down their tools to take up better-paid and more prestigious jobs in hotels inevitably began to compare their situation with that of the affluent tourists they encoutered every day. Their feeling of resentment was exacerbated by the fact that tourism had brought not only work to the islands but also a considerable increase in the cost of living, affecting not only luxury items but also basic commodities which the Seychellois themselves needed on a day-to-day basis.

As wages rose to meet the new standard of living and higher import duties were levied on goods, prices for tourists continued to soar and those "little extras" (taxis, an evening drink at the bar, etc.) suddenly represented a significant expense. The once flourishing high-class tourism of the Seychelles began to crumble. Add a number of political imponderabilia and the picture is complete. The impressive figures of 1979 fell by more than a third by 1982, when only some 47,000 visitors came to the islands.

Fresh insight and renewed energy pave the way for recovery

Recognizing the importance of tourism (it was now the Seychelles' undisputed primary source of foreign exchange and a mainstay of both the economy and the labour market), the government could not simply sit back and allow trends to run their natural course. When it was considered appropriate to do so, the management of hotels was taken over, facilities refurbished and brought into line with market norms, and price categories restructured – again in accordance with international standards. New partners whose role it would be to promote tourism were sought and found (whereby it must be said that the oft-cited principle of "quality tourism" was at times put to one side for the sake of expediency). In addition, it was decided that the services of Air Seychelles (up to this point restricted to inter-island traffic) should be extended to include international flights to and from Europe. The problem of those ever more costly "extras" was also dealt with in a most resolute manner, the government leading the way with the relinquishment of the airport charge of SR 100, which so many visitors had found objectionable. Even when tourism began to pick up again in the late 1980s, this levy was not reintroduced.

The Seychelles did not have to wait long to reap the rewards of their concerted action: in 1983 the number of visitors climbed back to 55,000, in 1985 it crossed the 72,000 mark and in 1988 even bettered the "dream figure" of 1979 when it reached a total of over 80,000. In line with this positive trend, earnings from tourism rose to previously unknown height, amounting to around thirty times the profits made in international trade. Which all goes to show just how important tourism is to the Seychelles – and just how vulnerable the island republic would be should tourism wane.

Having recognized this fact, it is now intended that the quality of Seychelles "goods" be further improved – without, however, allowing price (for the most part state controlled) to run wild. A long-term programme of hotel renovation and building is already underway. Short-term measures aimed at promoting tourism have also been undertaken. Take, for example, hire cars. At the beginning of 1988 only 520 out of a possible 700 hire car licences had been taken out. Existing stocks were neither replenished nor renewed, the main obstacle here being the high import tax levied on new cars. The solution to this problem was found without further ado in May 1988, when the import tax on cars intended for hire was halved for a limited period of time. So it was that the supply of cars could be made good relatively quickly and the fleets modernized: in accordance with the new stipulations, hire car licences are only granted on vehicles which are no more than three years old.

The tourist industry (hotel enterprises, travel agencies and the like) provide work and a living for almost 14 % of the islands' gainfully employed. Were we to consider those jobs which are indirectly linked to tourism, the figure would be much higher, of course. Every time you sit down to eat in a restaurant, step into a taxi, or purchase a Seychelles souvenir, you are making a contribution to the "indirect income from tourism".

The majority of holidaymakers on the islands come from Europe. Of the 84,184 visitors registered in 1988, a total 64,184 (i.e. around 76 %) were Europeans. In 1989 the European share rose to almost 80 % (68,613 out of a total 86,093). A number of nations vie for the leading positions in the statistics. In 1988 and 1989, the British (only fourth in 1985) edged the French from the head of the table (a position they had held for several years). Italian visitors have long been at home in third place, a comfortable distance ahead of the West Germans (who once headed the league; the drop in numbers of Germans shows what a difference less convenient flight connections can make).

As with every holiday destination, the ease with which the Seychelles are reached plays a decisive role in the selection process –the numer of visitors form Italy rose rapidly after direct flights (on a seasonal basis) were introduced there. Both European and North American visitors can now take advantage of direct Air Seychelles links with London, Frankfurt, Paris and Rome.

For those travelling on to Praslin, that journey has now been made much more convenient by the installation of equipment facilitating night flights. Visibility problems no longer preclude take-offs and landings at dawn and dusk, which means that stopovers in Mahé can often be avoided. (See also "Flights to the Seychelles" in the Useful Information section, pp. 156-164.)

Looking to the future

All the facts and figures quoted in the text (and in the table below) make one thing quite clear: the volume of visitors to the Seychelles represents an infinitesimal fraction of the millions of tourists who descend yearly upon the likes of the Mediterranean islands – first and foremost, Majorca. It would therefore be quite misplaced to talk of "mass tourism" on the Seychelles; nor should it be feared as a possible future development. In a five-year plan (finalized in 1989), the Seychelles dicided upon an strict policy of moderation in touristic development. In the period up to 1994, for example, the numer of hotel beds on the main islands of Mahé, Praslin and La Digue is not to exceed 4,000 (in 1989 the figure stood at almost 3,500 beds). Even allowing for this increase in capacity, holidaymakers have no reason to fear being packed into the islands like sardines. New hotels are to be limited to 100 beds and, wherever possible, are to be built on thus-far undeveloped beaches. Moderation in things touristic does not, of course, apply only to aforementioned main islands (where capacity is already greatest) It is considered even more important in the case of the other, smaller islands, which really are "away from it all". True to the official maxim, the aim will always be to preserve the "clear air, clean water and unspoilt landscape of the Seychelles".

Kaleidoscope of Seychelles Visitors
Taken from "Tourism and Migration Statistics" (Seychelles).

Visitors from:	1983	1985	1988	1989
Great Britain and Ireland	4,065	9,837	19,935	19,346
France	8,820	12,174	14,384	16,278
Italy	5,667	11,444	14,684	15,175
West Germany	9,759	10,085	5,581	7,371
Switzerland	6,192	5,637	3,126	2,882
Scandinavia	587	1,580	2,358	2,047
Réunion	1,179	1,744	1,348	2,081
East Africa	2,155	1,885	1,432	1,309
South Africa	2,020	2,001	2,947	5,057
Middle East	1,792	1,425	1,779	1,870
Japan	3,380	4,065	268	371
U.S.A.	1,694	1,329	1,624	1,913
Total	55,867	72,542	84,184	86,093

Bon Appetit à la Seychelloise

When Adam and Eve nibbled at that fateful apple in the Garden of Eden, that was it. No more paradise for us. We have to content ourselves nowadays with the Seychelles where things are not quite as they were in Eden. For, according to the locals, he who partakes of the breadfruit shall indeed return one day to the paradise islands of the Seychelles. You'll note that there is no reference to sin, although there are one ot two things, both on land and in the sea, for which one might be tempted to sin just a little perhaps!

Creative and imaginative – both words could be used to describe the skills of those Seychellois who prepare rare and tasteful dishes from the fruits of this fertile tropical soil and from the freshly-caught treasures of the sea. Don't be afraid to try something new, even if you aren't acquainted with all the ingredients. You'll find the essence of the Seychelles' Creole cuisine to be "artistry" resulting from French cooking harmonizing with the various influences of Chinese, African and British culinary traditions. That most of the menus will reflect basically French dishes is not surprising, as it was, after all, the French who first settled here in numbers over 200 years ago. The Indian influence provided an increased adeptness with spices, especially cinnamon, vanilla, pepper and ginger, as well as the taste for hot curries. The immigrants from the African mainland brought with them their expertise in the preparation of dishes featuring tropical fruits and vegetables, of which the breadfruit, yams, pumpkins and cassava are noteworthy. The habit of taking afternoon tea is a legacy of British rule – exported by them to all their colonial possessions – and is a tradion maintained all over the islands. But the British connection goes further – it's even been known for some Seychellois families to partake of a traditional English breakfast of bacon and eggs – especially on a Sunday morning!

Fish – thousands of unexpected variations

The kingpin of Seychelles cooking is fish – no doubt about it. You'll find it grilled, baked, roasted or boiled and always, of course, fresh and of the best quality. Quality *and* quantity... incredible amounts of fish are eaten in the Seychelles – far more than meat of

any kind. The latter is exorbitantly expensive and is bought by most people only on very special occasions. Hotels automatically feature meat on their daily bill of fare but this is far from a Seychelles norm.

The sheer number and variety of fish to be found in Seychelles waters is incredible. Should you like to see some of them "face to face", then a trip to the market in Victoria is definitely to be recommended. Alternatively you could wander down to the beach and watch as the fishermen come ashore with their catch: bonitos, parrotfish, red snapper, mackerel, tuna, swordfish, kingfish, blue marlin, cordonnier, job, bourgeois, rouget, vieille, shark, large and small mussels and such great delicacies as langouste/crayfish.

Fish gourmets should definitely make a point of adding the following to their list of culinary musts: grilled tuna or swordfish steaks; tuna soaked in a marinade containing cloves and a variety of herbs or in coconut milk; grilled bourgeois with ginger, onions and garlic; *daube (rougaille) de poisson* – braised fish (see recipe, p.114). Tasty fish curries are particularly typical of Creole cuisine: take for example, *carry zourite* (curried squid) or *carry do bonite* (curried bonito). Another speciality is fish wrapped in coconut or banana leaves and then steamed – *maquereau boucaner*.

Should you come across *kat-kat de bananas* on a menu, you can be sure you're looking at one of the most popular dishes ever to issue from the islands' kitchens. Order it and you'll be able to savour a unique concoction of fish, plantains and coconut milk. *Palourdes farcies* (stuffed clams) and *soupe de tectec* (a soup with tiny mussels) are also considered specialities of the Seychelles.

An exotic panoply of vegetables and fruits
Tastily-prepared fruits and vegetables are the other mainstay of Creole cooking – in the form of refreshing salads, delectable *chatinis* (assorted fruits and vegetables, shredded and sautéed in oil) and *daubes* (fruit cooked in coconut milk). To begin with, there are almost two dozen different types of banana – ranging from the small and very sweet varieties to record-breaking giants of 60 cm (almost 2 ft) in length. Besides plantains *(bananes St. Jacques)* – and leaving aside rice for the moment – sweet potatoes

(patate douce) and the breadfruit *(fruit à pain)* constitute the staple foods of the Seychelles people. Like potatoes, the starchy breadfruit and the root of the sweet potato can be eaten boiled, fried, baked or roasted and are a valuable source of nourishment. The latter is also true of the ever-popular *gallette*, made form cassava root. Another favourite of traditional Seychelles fare is *moucate*, the main ingredient of which is bananas.

The tantalizing aroma of fresh mangos, pineapples, papayas, guavas, melons, limes, coconuts, golden apples *(fruit ci terre)* and many, many more fruits will enchant again and again – as starters, salads, sweets or simply as a refreshing snack between meals.

Culinary Rarities
Very few visitors to the Seychelles will be lucky enough to taste the most famous delicacy among Seychellois desserts, namely the sweet jelly obtained from slightly underripe coco-de-mer nuts the "largest and heaviest seed of the vegetable kingdom". There is, however, another costly item which is more readily available and really should be tried by one and all – non-millionaires should treat themselves and splash out! "Millionaire's salad" owes its name to the fact that a palmiste palm has to be felled in order to procure the tender palm hearts needed for the dish.

The more daring among gourmets may well decide to try one or two of the Seychelles specialities which were dreamt up by islanders at times when meat was a rare delicacy. What are you supposed to think when a *carry de chauve-souris*, i.e. a curry made with bat meat, suddenly crops up on a menu? It's as well to know that what's on offer here is the meat of large fruit bats with an wingspan of about a metre. For their *fricassée d'oeufs d'oiseaux* and their *carry coco d'oeufs d'oiseaux*, chefs use the eggs of various terns; limited numbers of these eggs may be collected on certain islands at specific times of the year.

Turtle meat really is very tasty; for many years it was also the only kind of meat available on more remote islands. Nowadays, in order to protect the species, only male turtles may be caught for food, quotas are small and strictly regulated, and the season is short. Which goes to explain why turtle meat is so rarely served up at table these days – not even for special Creole festivities. And that most spectacular of Seychelles repasts, the *caille*, is as good as a thing of the past. Small wonder that this should be the case: the recipe calls for the meat of the turtle to be detached from the carapace but then left in its own huge natural "pot" to be cooked over a gentle fire for several hours. Some 200 years ago this might well have been one of the rare culinary pleasures enjoyed by pirates and early settlers – and certainly constituted a vital part of their diet – but now, in the light of growing concern for endangered species, recipes based on beef, pork or poultry are certainly more appropriate (and only slightly less tasty!). The latter usually take the form of ragouts, fricassées or hot curries and are served with *riz Creole* –a popular piquant preparation of rice with ginger, onions, garlic and vegetables. Try *carry de beouf riz Creole* or *carry de poulet au coco riz Creole* – you certainly won't be disappointed!

Thirst and fire quenchers

Hot spices are often employed in Creole cooking –highly spiced food is good for you in the tropics. But then you also have to know how to put out that fire in your mouth, and amongst the best remedies are the delicious sweet dishes Seychelles cuisine has to offer: cakes containing coconut such as *gateau coco* or *tarte au coco*; cakes made of sweet potato with a vanilla sauce, *geteau de patate sauce vanille*; *flan coco*, a kind of coconut pudding; caramelized bananas; a compote of any numer of exotic fruits; and, above all else, such delicious specialities as *nougat coco* or *fondant au coco*.

The fruits of the islands also provide a number of excellent thirst quenchers: lemon juice, mixed fruit juices (various combinations of pineapple, guava, mango, passion fruit and lime), and the traditional refreshment of the locals –the "milk" of the coconut. Fermented "fruit juices" should be treated with respect: a little too much of the likes of *calou* (made from the juice of young coconuts) or *bacca* (from pineapple juice) – the latter similar in taste to rum – will soon have an intoxicating, indeed pernicious, effect! Better to stick to the popular beer of the islands, "SeyBrew", which is brewed according to German recipes and is very similar in taste to quality German beers.

Soft drinks sold under such names as "SeyCola" and "SeyPearl" cannot

Recipes from the Seychelles – well worth trying at home

Daube de Poisson

(Stewed fish) serves 4.
800g (just under 2 lbs)
bourgeois, vieille
or similar fish
1 onion
1 tomato
2 to 3 cloves of garlic
fresh ginger
oil, flour
salt, pepper, thyme,
tomato puree.

Cut the fish into 2.5 cm (1 inch) cubes, roll in flour and then deep fry. Put to one side. Peel onion and cut into slices; slice tomato. Peel garlic and ginger; crush the garlic and grate the ginger finaly.

Heat some oil in a frying pan, add onion and tomato; cover, fry lightly then add some water and allow to simmer. Add the deep-fried fish, tomato puree, garlic, ginger and thyme. Season to taste and simmer for 15-20 minutes. Serve hot, with rice and salad or chatini.

Chatini de Cocos

Serves 4
2 whole coconuts
or 500g (1.1 lbs) of
grated coconut
1 onion
3 fresh peppermint
leaves / pinch of
allspice
juice of one lemon
or lime
1 sachet of saffron
salt, pepper and oil.

Open the coconuts and grate the white meat. Peel the onion and cut into strips. Finely chop the peppermint leaves; crush the allspice (if using whole seeds).

Heat some oil in a casserole dish, brown the onions and add the saffron. Add the grated coconut and allspice. Season with salt, pepper and the chopped peppermint. Simmer for 4 or 5 minutes, stirring regulary. Remove from heat and add lemon or lime juice.

Nougat Coco

400g (14 oz) grated
coconut
400g (14 oz) sugar
0.2l (⅓ pint) water
2 fl. ozs. oil
pulp of one vanilla pod
grated nutmeg.

Add the sugar to the water in a pot, allow to dissolve, then bring to boil. Add the grated coconut and simmer gently, stirring the while, until the mixture turns a mid-brown colour (takes time!). Remove from heat and season with the vanilla and nutmeg. Pour the mixture onto an oiled tray and spread flat. Allow to stand for a least two hours, then cut into inch squares and serve as petits fours.

always boast the same high standards. Tea, on the other hand, can; it will usually come from plantations in the Seychelles. Another excellent hot thirst quencher is called *citronella* and is brewed from fresh lemon grass. If this tea is not offered as an alternative to the (usually fairly mediocre) coffee served, for example, at the end of the evening meal, do ask whether it would be possible to try it at some point. You never know, maybe the head waiter will be only too pleased to muster up the necessary raw materials –from his garden at home, if need be!

A final point: wines and spirits will be available in good hotels and restaurants. Choice will be limited but sufficient; however, as this is an imported product, price will not be exactly low. In addition, selection, storage and serving of wine mean very little to all but the wealthiest of Seychellois –so you may well find that the wine that is served (and how it is served) leaves something to be desired.

Accommodation

Once you have decided that the Seychelles are going to be your next holiday destination, you will be faced with the question of accommodation. On the one hand, the fairly wide choice available on the islands allows for a degree of flexibility which can only be welcomed; on the other, however, it quite often means that one is spoilt for choice. Immediately one has to decide between two basic categories, each quite different in style, each catering to quite different tastes.

The larger hotels offer all the facilities (with regard to sports and entertainment) that one expects from such establishments. The alternative would be to opt for one of the smaller guesthouses: these are run informally and the atmosphere in them is in keeping with this. The final decision really does depend upon one's personal preferences and expectations of a holiday.

The aformentioned guesthouses could almost be considered a speciality of the Seychelles. They are to be found on the three islands where the vast majority of tourists are concentrated, i.e. Mahé, Praslin and La Digue, and their relativ importance becomes clear if we compare their numbers with those of "regular" tourist hotels. While there are 28 medium and large hotels in the Seychelles, there is a total of 38 guesthouses. To give some iedea of the sizes of the various establishments: on Mahé, numbers of rooms in medium and large hotels range from 25 to some 200; on Praslin, one finds even smaller hotels; almost without exception, small hotels and guesthouses have 10 rooms or less, in many cases just 2 to 4.

Needless to say, by far the largest share of the total of almost 3,500 beds (1989) falls to the medium and large hotels. The role played by guesthouses may be minor (in numerical terms) but is nonetheless considerable, bringing as it does a measure of individuality to the topic of accommodation in the Seychelles. The same is true of the islands' cuisine –it's truly a delight to find that some masterpieces of Creole cooking are served in many a smaller establishment. A glance through the list of restaurant tips on pp. 127-129 should give some idea of the bill of fare. The quality of the food in a number of other guesthouses would easily justify their being included in such a list, but the size of the premises often means that they are unable to cater for nonresidential guests.

Most people who visit the Seychelles do so within the framework of a pakage deal offered by a tour operator (and usually including flight, transfer an accommodation). This being the case, detailed descriptions in catalogues usually provide ample information for the purpose of selecting accommodation. It's worth bearing in mind, however, that most operators have contracts with specific hotels only; guesthouses will be included in their programme to a greater or lesser degree depending on the nature of that programme, and some will never be featured at all.

For this reason, a summary of accommodation available in the Seychelles may well be of use to the visitor. All information is taken from Seychelles Tourist Board sources (1990). To give some idea of costs, and thus enable comparisons to be drawn between various establishments, a separate list of prices (in Seychelles rupees) is also included. Experience has shown that even in the case of price increases, no major alterations take place in the classifications of the various establishments. Space available here for the summary did not allow for the inclusion of special prices offered

by certain tour operators or dictated by seasonal "highs" and "lows"; nor was it possible to detail supplements levied (for example, for services on national holidays).

As a (very rough) guide to price in US$ and pound sterling, one can reckon that Seychelles rupees divided by 5 = 1 US$ and divided by 7 = 1 pound sterling. For the exact rate of exchange, see the foldout map at the back of the guide or enquire at any bank.

Selected Hotels

Of foremost importance to most Seychelles tourists (once, that is, a particular price range has been selected – or maybe even prior to that...) will be details of the characters and location of the various hotels. This aspect has therefore been stressed and details of sports facilities and other amenities left to the catalogue texts of travel agents and tour operators.

The hotels are listed according to their location, starting at the northwest coast of Mahé and moving clockwise round to the west coast, and at the northeast coast of Praslin and circling to the west coast.

Abbreviations: B = no. of beds;
R = no. of rooms;
S = no. of suites;
CH = no. of chalets or bungalows;
V...km = distance from Victoria in km.

Mahé – Northwest Coast
Auberge Club des Seychelles, Danzilles. Stands on an elevation between cliffs, with round bungalows, some of which are surrounded by gardens and stand between tall trees (i.e. are pleas-

antly cool!). Swimming pool directly at the coast, access to the open sea via ladder, good snorkelling. No sand beach. Lots of steps. Easy-going, relaxed atmosphere, ideally suited to the young and sporting. Disco on Fridays. R/CH. V 7 km.

Le Méridien Fisherman's Cove Hotel, Bel Ombre. Slightly elevated location at the western edge of Beau Vallon Beach. Pleasant bathing in the open sea (especially at ebb tide) just a few hundred metres from the hotel; the same is true of water sports. Rooms in the main building or in rows of bungalows in spacious gardens. First-class establishment with discerning, international clientèle. 48 R/CH. V 6 km.

Beau Vallon Bay Hotel, Beau Vallon. Situated right on Beau Vallon Beach (shady takamaka trees), large hotel garden with palms. Two-storey hotel is Y-shaped, which means farthest rooms are at quite a distance. Lively, sporting asmosphere; wide range of entertainments (including casino). 184. R. V 5 km.

Coral Strand Hotel, Beau Vallon. Three-storey building shaped like a horseshoe; terrace for sun bathing, pool bar (a popular meeting place!) and restaurant directly at the beach. Adjacent to Underwater Centre. Easy-going clientèle, mostly of sporting inclination. Regular evening entertainment in the (disco) bar or at the pool. 102 R. V 5 km.

Northolme Hotel, Glacis. Built on an elevated rock spur beside a sandy bay (good bathing), surrounded by shady takamaka trees. Colonial-style furnishings. Diving centre based in the hotel; very good snorkelling area adjacent.

Rather conservative but stimulating clientèle. 19 R. V 8 km.

Sunset Beach Hotel, Glacis. Small, top-class bungalow hotel built on a bizarrely-shaped cliff overlooking a small bay with sand beach and good snorkelling nearby. Tasteful, "private" atmosphere. 18 R., 6 S. V 9 km.

Vista Bay Club, Glacis. Hotel complex consisting of two-storey buildings built in a series of terraces on a slope. The restaurant and small beach at the other side of the coast road are reached via a pedestrian bridge. Snorkelling an diving (instruction) at the hotel. Suitable for a secluded kind of holiday in a relaxed, informal atmosphere. 34 R, spacious. V 11 km.

Mahé – East Coast
Reef Hotel, Anse aux Pins. Parallel to beach; accommodation in long, two-storey complex built parallel to the beach. Sporting atmosphere, a result of the many water sports on offer and the 9-hole golf course (at the other side of the coast road). 150 R. V 14 km. Airport 4 km north of hotel (noise is not a problem).

Mahé – Southwest Coast
The Plantation Club, Val Mer. Spacious complex on the site of a former coconut plantation directly on a bay with a long sand beach. Well-appointed, spacious rooms and suites with terrace or balcony in two-storey guesthouses. A first-class hotel (international standards). Nightclub and casino 206 R/S. V 29 km/45 mins.

Mahé – West Coast
Le Méridien Barbarons Beach Hotel, Barbarons. Located in extensive park-

like grounds, built in open, "airy" style typical of the Seychelles, directly on a long sand beach. Two-storey building with guest rooms. Informal, elegant atmosphere with a sporting touch. Discerning clientèle. 125 R. V 12 km.

Equator Grand Anse Residence Hotel, Grand Anse. Top-class hotel built on various levels on a rocky slope directly at the sea. Accommodation solely in spacious suites, each comprising bedroom living area, garden and/or terrace. Freshwater swimming pool midway between coast and highest point; pool at the coast is filled with seawater. The hotel has a small sand beach; Grand Anse's long beach is a ten-minute walk away. Lots of steps. Watersports centre in Anse à la Mouche (some 10 km away, free transfer). Under Italian management, highly-acclaimed Italian cuisine: both factors account for the presence of a large number of Italian guests. Lots of entertainment on offer, for example a disco. 59 S. V 13 km.

Seychelles Sheraton Hotel, Port Glaud. The former Mahé Beach Hotel. After large-scale renovations in 1987, it was reopened as a top-class hotel. Exposed location atop the rocky coastline; all the (very comfortable) rooms enjoy an extensive view. Tropical garden between hotel and beach. Own watersports centre on Thérése Island, which lies opposite the hotel across the bay. Regular ferry connection. Discerning international clientèle. 161 R/11 S. V 15 km.

Praslin – Northeast and East Coast.
La Réserve. Anse Petite Cour. Built directly on an narrow stretch of beach,

this spacious bungalow complex lies opposite Curieuse Island. Bungalows comfortably furnished, with terrace. Easy-going, informal atmosphere. Acclaimed cuisine, the emphasis on Creole. Restaurant on piles built across the beach and out into the sea. 3 R/12 CH.

Paradise Hotel, Anse Volbert. Palm-thatched chalets in extensive grounds. Easy access (across the coast road) to the long, wide beach of Anse Volbert. 42 CH.

Village du Pêcheur, Anse Volbert. Small, clean bungalow complex in the style of a Creole village. Stands directly on Anse Volbert. Air and light are let into the rooms only by way of doors. 9 CH.

Chauve Souris Island Lodge, on the island of the same name – the tiniest of the Seychelles islands to be "developed" for tourism. Tropical vegetation and granite boulders surround palm-thatched bungalows. Arguably the most luxurious rooms to be found in the Seychelles. Lies just off Anse Volbert (a few hundred metres offshore, can be reached on foot at low tide) 4 R.

Praslin Beach Hotel, Côte d'Or. Bungalow complex arranged in a semi-circle around a large swimming pool. Not far from the beach at Anse Volbert (access over a seldom-used road). Guests are generally of the sporting, easy-going kind. Bungalows in rows; some have balcony, others terrace. 60 R.

Côte d'Or Lodge, Côte d'Or. The bungalows of this hotel are grouped between coconut palms directly on the beach, where there are plenty of opportunities for water sports. The individual bungalows and the main building (with restaurant and bar) are thatched with palm leaves – a practice which is typical of the island. 28 R. in 14 CH.

L'Archipel, Anse Gouvernement. Secluded hotel complex built in colonial chalet style, on a slope at a narrow beach. Extensive view from all rooms and from the restaurant in the main building out over Anse Volbert and as far as Curieuse Island. Rooms are spacious, furnishings tasteful and solidly-made. Lots of steps. As far as living comfort and cuisine are concerned, geared towards a demanding clientèle. 16 R. in 8 CH.

Praslin – South Coast
Chateau de Feuilles, Pointe Cabris. Stands on high ground surrounded by a lush tropical garden. Built in the elegant style that its name suggests. The top-quality cuisine (by any international standards) is in line with the luxuriousness of this country house. 10 R/CH.

Praslin – West Coast
Flying Dutchman, Grand Anse. Bungalow hotel with a long tradition, built on both sides of the coast road. The freestanding bungalows (with verandah) are scattered throughout a spacious garden; the restaurant is at the beach. Ideal place for a more secluded kind of holiday. 13 CH.

Maison des Palmes, Grand Anse. Hotel complex directly on the beach. Spacious semi-detached bungalows, each with its own verandah. Pleasant,

airy restaurant; good Creole cooking. Swimming pool. Boat trips to Cousin Island start out from here. Informal, sporty atmosphere. 16 CH.

La Digue
La Digue Logde, Anse la Réunion. Well-known Grégoire's Island Lodge (pointed gable chalets directly on the beach) was joined with the Creole "Yellow House" and with the bungalows of La Digue Island Lodge (on the other side of the village road) to form La Digue Lodge. The large, lofty restaurant on the sand beach is built of wood (local architecture). Large swimming pool. Pleasant, relaxed atmosphere with a sporting touch. 35 R/CH.

Felicité
Felicité Island, hotel run by La Digue Lodge. Two houses built in typical Seychelles style for a holiday "away from it all". Plenty of opportunities for water sports, but also for tennis. 4 R.

Silhouette
Silhouette Island Lodge, La Passe. Bungalow complex set in a palm grove directly on the beach. Spacious rooms with sturdy rustic furnishings in detached bungalows. Silhouette has a great deal to offer nature lovers and hiking enthusiasts, combined with the tranquility resulting from its isolated location. 12 CH.

Frégate
The Plantation House. A former planter's house with four guest rooms and a large verandah, on which meals are also served. Remaining guest rooms are divided between an annexe and a bungalow on the nearby beach. Large rooms, albeit simply furnished. There's an impressive banyan tree in

front of the house. A tropical paradise, a refuge for the victims of stress. 10 R.

Bird Island
<u>Bird Island Lodge</u>. Bungalow complex in a palm grove directly on the coast, very close to the nesting area which has brought Bird Island its fame. Open-air restaurant with a view of the beach and sea. The palm-thatched bungalows are spacious and airy. Natural, easy-going atmosphere. 25 CH.

Denis Island
<u>Denis Island Lodge</u>. Bungalow complex in a palm grove; care was taken that ample space be left between the single bungalows. All buildings – including the openair restaurant with its high roof – are very spacious and typical of the local architecture (palm leaf thatching, for example). The couple who own the lodge cultivate a relaxed, unaffected atmosphere. All in all, geared towards a discerning clientèle. 25 CH.

Desroches/Amirantes
<u>Desroches Island Lodge</u>. Comfortably furnished lodge on the largest of the Amirantes. Each bungalow has its own verandah. Fully-equipped water sports centre, including facilities for diving and deep-sea fishing. Ideal for all water sports enthusiast. 20 CH.

<u>A tip when selecting a hotel:</u> all establishments within the "Seychelles Hotels" group allow guests to exchange accommodation and/or meals. Every guest of one of these hotels receives a "Fun Card" which ensures further special services and benefits.

Selected Guesthouses

(Island by island, guest houses in alphabetical order)

Mahé
<u>Auberge d'Anse Boileau</u>, southwest coast. Row of palm-thatched bungalows in a tropical garden. The sea at the other side of the road; beach just a few minutes away on foot. Restaurant "Chez Philos" enjoys a widespread culinary reputation. 8 R.

<u>Auberge Lous XVII</u>, La Louise. Attractively situated on a height overlooking the islands of the Ste. Anne Marine National Park. Beautiful tropical garden, excellent restaurant "Suisse". 5 R.

<u>Casuarina Beach</u>, Anse aux Pins. Directly on the beach, surrounded by a lush tropical garden. Good food (Creole, European). Reef Hotel Golf Course nearby. 12 R.

<u>Chateau d'Eau</u>, Barbarons/west coast. Former planter's house with its own beach; well-kept garden. Renowned Creole-French cuisine. Sophisticated yet friendly atmosphere. 5 R.

<u>Coco d'Or</u>, Beau Vallon. Small, comfortable modern complex some 200 m from Beau Vallon Beach. Creole cuisine. 8 R.

<u>L'Islette</u>. Bungalow complex on the tiny island of the same name off the west coast. Spacious rooms, rustic character. Quality cuisine, plenty of variety. Robinson Crusoe-style existence but with comfort. 4 R.

Lazare Picault, Baie Lazare. Palm-thatched round bungalows between granite and the green of tropical vegetation. On an elevation overlooking Baie Lazare. Excellent Creole restaurant. 14 CH.

Manresa, Anse Etoile. Modern guesthouse directly on the northeast coast. All rooms enjoy view of Victoria and the islands of the Ste. Anne Marine National Park. 5 R.

Panorama, Mare Anglaise. Modern guesthouse located above Beau Vallon Beach, panorama view of the bay. 8 R.

Pension Bel Air, Bel Air. Former colonial house with view of Victoria's harbour. Highly-acclaimed Creole cuisine. 7 R.

Residence Bougainville, southeast coast. Former plantation house surrounded by tropical garden, some 20 km (12 miles) from Victoria and 1.5 km (just under a mile) form Anse Royale (on the bay of the same name). Refined European and Creole cuisine. 7 R.

Rose Cottage, Pointe au Sel. Guesthouse run on informal lines; on a sheltered bay on the east coast. Swimming and snorkelling. 3 R.

Sunrise, Mont Fleuri. Modern family guesthouse in Seychellois style on the outskirts of Victoria. Creole and Chinese cooking are specialities. 7 R.

Le Tamarinier, Bel Ombre (North Mahé). Modern guesthouse; tranquil; shady trees. 11 R.

Praslin
Indian Ocean Fishing Club, Grand Anse. Chalet hotel directly at the beach; geared towards sporting activities. Point of departure for boat trips to Cousin Island (bird sanctuary). 12 CH.

Grand Anse Beach Villas, Grand Anse. Small pension built in chalet style directly on the beach on the outskirts of Grand Anse. 8 R.

The Britannia, Grand Anse. Modern guesthouse; informal atmosphere. Restaurant offers Creole and Chinese bill of fare. 5 R.

La Digue
Choppy's Bungalows, Anse la Réunion. Simple yet appealing stone bungalows near the beach. Good Creole cooking. 4 R.

Apartments and Bungalows for Self-Catering Holidays

Mahé
Blue Lagoon, Anse à la Mouche. Bungalow komplex on one of southwest Mahé's most beautiful beaches. Ideal conditions for all water sports. Spacious bungalows with three rooms for 4 – 6 people. 4 CH.

Michel Holiday Apartments, Le Rocher. On the coast road between Victoria and the airport. Spacious living area-cum-bedroom for 1 – 4 people. 16 apartments.

Vacoa Village, Beau Vallon. Spanish-style apartment complex on the northwest coast of Mahé. Studios and apartments are spacious and comfortable. Swimming pool. 9 R/CH.

Hotels, Guesthouses, Apartments

Source: Hotel listing 1990
Prices in SR per person per day

Rooms: 1 = single; 2 = double; 3 = three beds

	Bed/Breakfast			Half Board			Full Board		
	1	2	3	1	2	3	1	2	3
Mahé – Hotels									
Auberge Club des Seychelles	700	875	1155	820	1095	1390	-	-	-
Le Meridien Barbarons Beach	705	920	1140	850	1210	1575	-	-	-
Beau Vallon Bay	890	1055	1325	960	1260	1580	-	-	-
Coral Strand	835	950	-	1000	1280	-	-	-	-
Equator Grand Anse Residence	630	655	790	820	900	1170	-	-	-
Le Meridien Fisherman's Cove	770	990	1315	935	1320	1810	-	-	-
Northolme Hotel	800	1070	-	960	1265	-	-	-	-
Reef Hotel	660	870	955	760	1020	1225	-	-	-
Seychelles Sheraton	800	1020	-	-	-	-	-	-	-
Sunset Beach	800	880	-	990	1200	-	1090	1435	-
Plantation Club	660	820	900	700	1020	1200	-	-	-
Vista Bay Club	600	770	-	700	850	-	-	-	-
Mahé – Guesthouses, smaller hotels									
Auberge d'Anse Boileau	425	450	475	525	650	775	625	850	975
Auberge Louis XVII	302	407	-	358	522	-	407	599	-
Beaufond Lane	175	250	-	-	-	-	-	-	-
Beau Vallon Bungalows	175	275	-	-	-	-	-	-	-
Carefree	220	300	375	300	425	615	380	585	855
Casuarina Beach	325	420	600	400	575	675	-	-	-
Calypha	125	200	-	180	310	-	-	-	-
Chateau d'Eau	500	600	-	640	880	-	-	-	-
Chez Jean	250	300	-	300	400	-	-	-	-
Coco d'Or	395	470	-	435	580	-	-	-	-
Harbour View	220	320	-	260	380	-	300	450	-

Hilltop	250	350	500	–	–	–	–	–
La Retraite	132	210	–	–	180	290	–	–
La Rousette	230	310	390	–	290	430	–	–
Lalla Panzi	200	265	–	560	260	380	–	–
Lazare Picault	300	395	–	–	370	520	–	–
Le Niol	175	235	–	–	210	295	230	350
La Tamarinier	295	450	–	–	360	530	–	–
Les Manguiers	Whole house (1-3 pers.) with breakfast SR 250 per person per day							
L'Islette	–	450	–	–	225	550	–	–
Manresa	275	325	–	–	305	445	405	550
Marie Antoinette	125	250	–	–	–	–	–	–
North Point	Self-catering; SR 200 per person (for at least 2; min. stay 3 nights)							
Panorama	–	350	450	–	350	475	590	775
Pension Bel Air	310	420	550	–	380	560	760	590
Residence Bougainville	285	375	525	–	340	485	635	–
Sea Breeze	260	330	–	–	–	–	–	–
Sunrise	200	275	–	–	260	395	320	515
Villa Madonna	200	240	–	–	–	–	–	–
Villa Napoleon	196	308	–	–	–	–	–	–

Mahé – Self-catering apartments

Bel Ombre Holiday Villas	SR 280 whole house (4 pers.); SR 380 whole house (6 pers.)
Blue Lagoon Chalets	SR 4610 per week (full chalet = 4 pers.); SR 2305 per week (half chalet = 2 pers.)
Michel Holiday Apartments	SR 2500 per week (studio; bed/breakfast)
Vacoa Village	SR 735 (studio); SR 875 (1-bedroom apartment); SR 1085 (2-bedroom apartment)

	Bed/Breakfast			Half Board			Full Board		
	1	2	3	1	2	3	1	2	3
Praslin – Hotels									
Chateau de Feuilles	1700	800	–	1300	900	–	–	–	–
Chauve Souris Island Lodge	–	1100	1050	–	–	–	–	–	–
Côte d'Or Lodge	590	780	–	710	1030	1420	790	1200	1680
Cabanes des Pêcheurs	250	300	350	310	420	480	–	–	–
Flying Dutchman	655	825	955	745	1010	1195	–	–	–
Colibri	275	370	–	320	500	–	–	–	–
Maison des Palmes	450	560	695	540	698	804	600	820	990
La Reserve	600	740	–	750	1010	–	–	–	–
L'Archipel	720	780	–	880	1100	–	–	–	–
Paradise Hotel	485	700	925	570	880	1320	–	–	–
Praslin Beach Hotel	610	770	930	695	935	1105	–	–	–
Village de Pêcheur	575	700	–	654	825	–	–	–	–
Praslin – Guesthouses									
Britannia	200	280	–	270	290	–	330	550	–
Grand Anse Beach Villas	200	270	350	–	–	–	–	–	–
Indian Ocean Fishing Club	–	–	–	470	600	–	–	–	–
Orange Tree House	125	225	–	–	–	–	–	–	–
La Digue – Hotels, Guesthouses									
La Digue Lodge	–	–	–	684	978	–	738	1080	–
Choppy's Bungalows	–	–	–	255	360	–	320	480	–
Bernique	200	250	–	275	350	–	–	–	–
Various Islands – Lodges									
Bird Island	–	980	–	–	–	–	–	–	–
Denis Island	–	–	–	–	–	–	1100	1600	–
Desroches	–	–	–	–	–	–	849	1194	1791
Felicité	–	–	–	–	–	–	–	–	–
Frégate	–	–	–	–	–	–	745	970	–
Silhouette	–	–	–	–	–	–	–	–	–

Felicité: Full board (incl. drinks) SR 3000 (1 pers.) – SR 12240 (8 pers.)

Silhouette: Standard bungalow SR 555 per person per day; Executive bungalow SR 675 per person per day

Entertainment...
...and Gastronomy

Entertainment in the Seychelles is something written with a capital E, more often disregarded as not really part of the scene here. It all depends on who is entertaining, who is being entertained, and where things are happening. The main island Mahé, for example, clearly offers a deal more than the smaller islands of the archipelago. For those who set no great store by entertainment, the latter will certainly provide all the peace and quiet they could ever wish for.

In an assessment of the entertainment on offer in the Seychelles, a great deal depends upon the expectations and demands of the individual. Anyone who has set their heart upon evenings spent away from the hotel – dropping into a bar, maybe into a number of different bars, dancing and having fun into the early hours – is bound to be disappointed.

Another important point is our understanding of entertainment. The programmes of music and (in some cases) dance offered by hotels in the evening most certainly come under the category of entertainment, but after the first week of one's holiday leave something to be desired – be it only a change! With luck you'll have the chance to see a performance of a *camole* show or *séga* cabaret, both featuring Creole-style music, song and dance. (Jocelyn Perreau, a Mauritian-born entertainer who is married to a Seychellois and now resident on the islands, is a most talented artiste whose performances can be considered exemplary.)

When on the look-out for a possible evening's entertainment be sure to consult the notice posted in most hotels and business frequented by tourists. Of late there has been a welcome increase in the number of guest performances (musicians and dance groups of international calibre) being organised in the Seychelles. Most take place in Victoria, so it's necessary to think about transport to the capital.

For those who decide somewhat more impulsively upon a night out there are discos – there are quite a number to choose from at weekends; the choice during the week is more limited. Here, too, you'll find that there are special events from time to time so it's as well to keep eyes and ears open; the daily newspaper *Nation* (available in the mornings form many hotel receptions) often gives notice of such events. The following is a selection of discos which are very popular with both locals and holiday-makers: the discotheque in the Auberge Club des Seychelles, Danzilles (northwest coast); in Le Surcouf, Pointe Conan (northeast coast); in the Equator Hotel (west coast); and in the Au Katiolo in Anse aux Pins (east coast, near the airport), where one can also eat quite well and then has free entry into the disco.

Diversion of a more sophisticated kind can be found in the casino of Beau Vallon Bay Hotel. There are one-armed bandits for the more modest gambler and roulette, blackjack and baccarat for those who feel their luck is really in. Moving somewhat farther afield, there's another casino down on the southwest coast – at the Plantation Club, Val Mer.

While on the topic of entertainment, we should finally also mention the fashion shows which are held from time to time on the islands and the possibility of taking a "Starlight Cruise" in a schooner around north Mahé – camtole music on board and then the sounds of moutia to accompany the barbecue on Round Island. And that would indeed be that – were it not for the pleasure of eating and drinking in the Seychelles.

A Short Compendium – "Eating Out"

For those in the know there's never any doubt: eating out (i.e. away from your hotel) is an absolute must in the Seychelles. This is in no way meant as a criticism of the mostly excellent food served up in the larger hotels and smaller guesthouses of the islands. Still, certain concessions do have to be made to the eating habits of an establishment's international clientèle and this is often at the expense of the piquant seasoning of Creole cuisine.

Hot spicy Creole dishes will certainly not be everyone's favourite; many will remain faithful fo French or Indian, Italian or Chinese cuisine – and will be pleased to find that there are good restaurants specializing in all four styles of cooking (and representing various price ranges). The truth is, of course, that all four of these "greats" made a sizeable contribution to the development of Creole cooking.

Eating out can, however, easily turn into a fairly costly business. I hasten to add that it is not the food itself which is so expensive – a simple but generous and delicious midday meal need cost no more than SR 50 (an evening meal will usually be more expensive since many restaurants offer special prices at midday). On the other hand, it's no problem at all to spend a very pleasant evening in a high-class restaurant and arrive at a bill of something like SR 180 per person. If you keep to the happy medium, however, (and this corresponds with price levels in most good restaurants) you can reckon with between SR 75 and SR 110 per person per evening meal.

Compared with the meal itself, it is wine which represents quite the most costly item on any restaurant bill. While it is possible to buy $^1/_2$ litre of house wine in a carafe for around SR 40, as soon as one moves to bottled wines (be they French or South African) the prices rise steeply. This being the case, it is accepted practice everywhere that the local beer (much more reasonably priced and very tasty) be ordered with a meal instead of wine.

While on the subject of costs, it should be remembered that many recommended restaurants are situated at a fair distance from the most popular tourist hotels. Since the schedules of local buses are geared towards the working population – and therefore tend to close down as of 7 p.m. –

you'll be dependent upon a taxi as a means of transport (unless, that is, you have hired a car). It's as well to keep these extras in mind, especially as supplements in force after 8 p.m. mean that charges increase quite appreciably. For more details, see "Useful Information/Taxis" p.160.

One decision with regard to eating will have been made long before your first restaurant visit in the Seychelles: namely that of whether to book full board or half board. Opting for half board means that a portion of basic funds will automatically be available for eating out – and one is, of course, more flexible. But even if you have decided that full board is the more practical solution – for example, because your hotel enjoys a secluded location – do forego a meal from time to time in order to eat out – it really is a pleasure you shouldn't miss.

Guests of establishments within the "Seychelles Hotels" group have another way of ensuring variety in the bill of fare they enjoy. The group's "FUN card" enables holders to exchange meals in four hotels on Mahé and three on Praslin. More about this in the chapter "Accommodation", p.115.

Restaurant Tips

In compiling the following selection the decision was made only to include those restaurants which have specialized in a particular type of food, thereby differing from the restaurants of larger hotels which cater to the tastes of a wide clientèle. That the restaurants of a number of guesthouses should be included is in no way inconsistent with this – the specialities they offer and their ambience more than merit a mention.

As with any kind of selection, the following is based on subjective appraisal – personal impressions and experiences – and cannot hope to be immune to the kind of fluctuations in quality which can occur when management and/or kitchen staff change. The best idea is to enquire about up-to-date tips once you arrive in the Seychelles. And particularly in the case of smaller restaurants, be sure to phone in good time to reserve a table with the desired number of places.

In the restaurants listed a normal midday of evening meal (including a number of courses) should cost up to around SR 160 for two people (not including drinks). Where there is a considerable deviation from this, prices are given in brackets.

Mahé

Baobab Pizzeria, Beau Vallon. Tel: 47167. Small restaurant directly on the beach of Beau Vallon, north of the Hotel Coral Strand. Italian specialities, in particular pizza and pasta.

Bel Air Guesthouse, Victoria. Tel: 22616. Small and simple guesthouse, merits the status of an insider tip on the strength of the excellent Creole food (only in the evenings). Very friendly people.

Chez Philos, Anse Boileau. Tel: 76660. Restaurant in the Auberge d'Anse Boileau guesthouse in southwest Mahé; small and rustic, has gained recognition for its culinary achievements, especially with fish and seafood.

Le Corsaire, Bel Ombre. Tel: 47141. Reputable restaurant, specializes in quality French cuisine. Located directly on the northwest shore. View out over the ocean as far as Silhouette. (SR 350-400)

Islander Restaurant, Anse à la Mouche. Tel: 71289. Small restaurant in southwest Mahé, view over the bay. Fish dishes, especially grilled fish, are the speciality.

Le Kakatwa, Anse Etoile. Tel: 41327. On the coast north of Victoria, restaurant specializes in Creole cuisine, especially seafood dishes. Indian cuisine is also good (SR 200-300).

Lazare Picault, Baie Lazare. Tel: 71117. Stands atop a granite cliff with a fine view of the Baie Lazare, southwest Mahé. Restaurant in guesthouse of the same name is well known for its delicious Creole specialities.

Lobster Pot, Pointe Canon. Tel: 41376. Stands directly on the coast, north of Victoria; view out to sea. Specialities of the house: seafood and grilled dishes à la Creole. (Evenings approx. SR 200; reasonably priced midday meals.)

Mandarin, Victoria (Revolution Av., corner Albert St.). Tel: 22818. Traditional Chinese food (Evenings approx. SR 170-180).

Marie Antoinette, Victoria (upper end of Revolution Ave.). Tel: 23942. Restaurant in old colonial house, Creole

specialities. One set Creole meal is offered each day – menu changes on a daily basis. Excellent quality, lots of atmosphere.

La Marmite, Victoria (Revolution Ave., near Quincy St.). Tel: 22932. Renowned for its Creole dishes, seafood.

La Moutia, La Misère. Tel: 44433. Reputable restaurant with a fine view of Victoria's harbour and the off-shore islands. International cuisine (SR 250-300).

La Perle Noire, Beau Vallon, opposite Hotel Coral Strand. Tel: 47046. Restaurant specializing in Creole and French cuisine. Pleasant covered terrace. (SR 300-350).

La Scala, Bel Ombre. Tel: 47535. Top-class restaurant built atop granite cliffs at the end of the coast road; skilful architecture. Exquisite Italian and French cuisine, wide selection of choice wines (Approx. SR 320-380).

Suisse Restaurant, Victoria. Tel: 44404. Known in particular for its fish dishes, restaurant is in the guesthouse Auberge Louis XVII, La Louise.

La Sirene, Anse aux Poules Bleues. Tel:71339. Small restaurant in southwest Mahé, located directly on the beach. Specialities: fish, seafood and *chauve-souris* (flying fox, a fruit bat). Plenty of atmosphere, fine view out to sea (Up to SR 250).

Pomme Cannelle, Anse aux Pins. *The* restaurant in which to enjoy Seychellois fare. Care is taken to uphold the traditions of the local cuisine, all in the historical atmosphere of a former planter's house in the Craft Village (SR 180-350).

Village Inn, Anse Royale. Tel: 76219. Restaurant on Anse Royale Bay (southeast coast); fine Creole food (SR 200-250).

Two good addresses for a snack in Victoria:

L'Admiral, "open air" restaurant in a side section of Independence House (entrance on Independence Av.). Popular place for lunch, moderate prices for set meals (up to SR 60 per person).

Pirates Arms, Independence Ave., probably the best-known restaurant in Victoria; popular meeting place. Wide selection of complete meals as well as inexpensive snacks (up to around SR 90 per person).

Praslin

Laurier, Anse Volbert. Tel: 32241. Small, simple restaurant with good Creole and European cuisine. Snacks, lunches and evening meals at moderate prices.

The remaining restaurants which can be recommended on Praslin are to be found for the most part in hotels and guesthouses around the island. First and foremost, the Chateau de Feuilles, high above Pointe Cabris in the southeast. Often dubbed the "culinary hub of the Seychelles", the restaurant is usually only open to guests of the hotel.

Seychelles Rhythms

The Seychellois love music, they love rhythm, and they love to dance. Music and dance have always – ever since the introduction of slavery over 200 years ago – been both an expression of *joie de vivre* and a plea for oblivion. And what might be called the African element of the Seychellois mentality has always been, and continues to be, dominant here, proving itself stronger even than the intellectual and cultural influence of France, the latter manifest in the preponderance of French in Seychelles Creole.

This duality of their cultural heritage is also reflected in the music of the islands: moutia and séga, both of African origin, dominate music in the Seychelles both on an everyday basis and when it comes to festivities on special occasions. Moutia is in fact considered to be at the root of all musical development in the Seychelles. Originally a rite, a prayer, it was transformed into a song by slaves. In the same way the slaves used dance to give expression to their sufferings and sorrows, but also to their hopes and dreams. The most popular setting for the moutia to be danced is in the flickering light of an outdoor fire, preferably at full moon, to the accompaniment of men and women singing in antiphony, and to the rhythmic beating of a large round drum.

Not unlike moutia, séga is probably better known to most as the "rhythm of Mauritius". The main difference between the séga of Mauritius and that of the Seychelles lies in the choice of percussion instrument. In the Seychelles the rhythmic accompaniment is beaten out on a drum made from the hollowed-out trunk of a coconut palm.

Few people nowadays will have the opportunity to see "original" versions of these dances. Impromptu "performances" are only really found as part of family celebrations or come about very spontaneously, i.e. as a rule when the locals are among themselves. Still, the truly commercialized performances, although exhibiting a strong show element, do in fact give some impression of the passion and power in the music. Séga has over the years acquired a more prominent role in the music of everyday life and this will be reflected in the programme of enter-

tainment on offer. One thing's for sure, Radio Seychelles never seems to tire of broadcasting modern hits which are clearly based on the traditional melodies and rhythms of the islands. No wonder, then, that old and young are happiest dancing to the same kind of stirring music.

Alongside this music of African origin, a French dance tradition has also been handed down in the shape of the contredanse. Introduced by French settlers, the contredanse usually is played by a camtole band made up of violin, accordion, banjo and drum. The contredanse has certainly stood the test of time; as an expression of high spirits and good cheer it is unbeatable and is therefore a great favourite at weddings and other celebrations.

Out and About in the Seychelles

After all that you will have read about the Seychelles you'll no doubt feel the inclination to be out and about on the islands – to see as much as possible, or at least to get to know something of the archipelago. This is easiest and most rewarding if you have chosen Mahé as your holiday base.

In the first place, there is more to see and experience on Mahé – it is after all the largest island of the group; in the second, it represents the "crossroads" of inter-island air and sea traffic, thus enabling visitors to "hop" quite easily from one island to the next. It really is important to take advantage of this opportunity, as it is

only by visiting around that one arrives at a more or less rounded picture of the true and manifold beauty of the Seychelles archipelago.

If we consider the extent of Mahé from the point of view of passable roads, then the island measures no more than 25 km (some 15 $^1/_2$ miles) from north to south and just 5 km (a little over 3 miles) from east to west. No problem, then, completing the round trip of the island in just one day – no need to hurry unduly either: if you're travelling around in a hired car you'll note that at the end of the day you've barely clocked up 100 km (62 miles). Still, such a "crash course" should be limited to one's first time around, when it is a question of gaining an overall picture of Mahé. The round trip detailed on p.136 was therefore not intended as an itinerary for a day trip but as an aid to orientation in the planing of a tour in a number of stages. It would, after all, be a pity if one were to "do" only two of the five possible routes crossing the island from east to west. Much like passes, all five roads make their way through the highlands of the interior before descending to the coast again, yet each is unique as far as the surrounding landscape is concerned. And,

let's face it, wouldn't it be a sin if one didn't take the time to enjoy the superb views from vantage points along the way, to linger for a while in charming villages, or to relax on one of the particularly beautiful beaches in the south of the island?

Bus tours, organised by local travel agents and the representatives of international tour operators, are to be recommended for those who appreciate an explanation of the landscape, places of interest, etc. as they go along (most guided tours will be conducted in English).

Most of the tour companies have fairly similar programmes. A day trip, for example, will usually include the highlights of Mahé, but will inevitably concentrate upon the capital Victoria and the coastal scenery of the south. Half-day tours cover either north Mahé (Victoria incl. museum and botanical garden, round trip along the coast to North Point and back), or south Mahé (Forêt Noire Rd. or La Misère Rd., southwest coast as far as Baie Lazare, Les Canelles Rd., east coast from Anse Royale back to Victoria).

A drawback of such an organised tour is that the most characteristic of Seychelles beaches – Anse Intendance above all – are not normally included. The only way to rectify this is to set off under your own steam. There are a number of ways of doing so, of course, the three most popular options being hire car, taxi and public bus.

Hire cars enjoy great popularity on Mahé. Vehicles on offer range from Minis to Mercedes; British and

Japanese makes do, however, dominate the field. Cars with automatic transmission are unfortunately as good as non-existent on the islands. "Topless" models such as the Suzuki jeep and the Minimoke head the popularity table. Both convey a great sense of

the fun and freedom of the open road – in the truest sense! If there's a sudden shower it's often not worth bothering trying to put up the hood – you'll be soaked to the skin before you're even half way there. Better ro rely upon the warm air to dry you off – which will happen in no time at all – as you drive along.

Besides Mahé, Praslin is the only other island where you'll find hire cars on offer: they are the only two islands which boast a road network worth speaking of. Most of the roads in the network of both islands are asphalted; if this is the case, they are classified "main roads" (in 1986, 162 km/100 miles of a total of 264 km/164 miles of road were included in this category). The surfacing (just a few years ago) of the stretch of road between Anse Boileau and Grand' Anse Village meant that the south Mahé circuit could at last be completed on asphalt. The road follows the coastline throughout almost its entire length (it turns inland, however, short of the southernmost tip of the island – Anse Intendance,

Police Bay – and skirts the peninsula west of Baie Lazare Village; secondary roads provide access to parts of both areas). The (almost entirely) coastal circuit is interrupted quite abruptly in the northwest, however, where there is a gap between Ternay and Bel Ombre/Danzilles – natural features of this particular coastal region stand in the way of a possible road link.

On the whole the roads are not conducive to speed, a factor that can only be in our interest as visitors. There's no reason to exceed either the general speed limit of 65 km/h (approx. 40 m.p.h.) or that of 40 km/h (25 m.p.h.) laid down for Victoria, other builtup areas on Mahé and the whole of Praslin. In light of the many twists and turns in the roads through the interior, and considering the possibility of sudden encounters with busses and trucks along narrow stretches, it's not a bad idea do drive even more slowly and carefully.

Traffic drives on the left in the Seychelles. Anyone not used to this might find it strange at first, but should have no real problems adapting (the fact that the drivers's seat is also on the "wrong" side often in fact helps make the mental adjustment). Far more vexing is the poor – or non-existent – signposting on Seychelles roads. So, for those doubtful cases, always have a good roadmap to hand (more detailed maps than those contained at the back of this guide are available on the islands: Mahé, scale 1 : 50,000; Praslin, 1 : 30,000).

Help can also usually be found in a police station – clearly marked as such and often conveniently located at crossroads, intersections or forks in the road. If you ask the way here you can be sure you'll be given reliable information. A case in point: the secondary road leading to the aforementioned Anse Intendance in south Mahé branches off the main road in Quatre Bornes opposite the police station there; the later turn-off for the approach to the bay is not marked in any way, however, so you'll need to consult your map for this.

If you don't feel too sure about finding your own way, you could always enquire about the possibility of hiring a car with driver. Should this idea appeal to you, your best bet may well be to consider option No. 2: taxis (see below).

N.B. Hire Car Bookings
Hire car bookings for the peak season (i.e. July and August and the period from the middle of December to the middle of January) should be made in good time – at best from home when you make your flight and hotel reservation. If you leave your booking until you're on the Seychelles, you may find yourself (at least at these very busy times of year) without any car at all, or obliged to accept a model you would not normally choose. And, since tariffs remain uniform, there's no material advantage in risking a last-minute booking anyway.

Taxi tours offer the same degree of freedom as a hire car with driver – flexibility in the choice of route and the security of knowing the driver knows the island inside out! The great advantage with taxis is that they're easier to hire and can be hired for much shorter periods of time, even for

just a couple of hours. Agreeing on a price shouldn't be difficult: using the official tariffs laid down by the Seychelles government for all fixed taxi routes, you'll be able to see whether the price asked is a fair one. Remember that waiting time will also be included. Your hotel reception will be able to assist you with information and/or estimates of cost in the light of past experience. See also "Useful Information, Taxis" p.160.

To give some idea of prices as they stood in 1989: on Mahé a half-day tour (approx. 5 hours) by taxi featuring a round trip from Victoria to the south cost SR 300; a 3-hour-tour of the same area starting out from Beau Vallon cost SR 210; on Praslin SR 200 were asked for a 2 $^1/_2$-hour tour of the island. Round trips which correspond to standard routes have fixed rates.

All in all, Seychellois taxis drivers have a very good record. As with all the Seychelles people, you'll be unlucky if you chance upon one who is sullen or unfriendly. Personal experience in the course of many visits and over a longer period of time has left a lasting and positive impression. Drivers called by hotel receptions for so-called outward journeys always proved to be alert and knowledgeable guides, volunteering suggestions as to where to stop off for the best photos, etc.

Public buses operated by the S.P.T.C. (Seychelles Public Transport Corporation) constitute the third – and by no means worst – option for getting to know Mahé under your own steam. They are certainly the most reasonably priced! There's not one journey to or from Victoria that will cost you more than SR 6, no matter whether you head into the far north or the deepest south. Even allowing for the fact that tickets do not permit passengers to change routes, travelling costs will be incredibly low: for example, from a hotel in Glacis to south Mahé and back you'll pay four SR 6 fares – a grand total of SR 24!

A total of 24 bus services link Victoria with Mahé's towns, villages and hotels, carry passengers along all the island's coast roads and even wind their way through the mountains of the interior. Easy, then, to reach places of interest, beautiful beaches and the like. And even if they're not directly on a bus route – as is the case with Anse Intendance, to mention it once again – the desired destinations are never that far away (20-25 minutes on foot to Anse Intendance, for example.

S.P.T.C. buses also run on two other islands in the Seychelles – there are four lines on Praslin, fares ranging between SR 2 and SR 6; the service on La Digue is a fairly recent innovation, standard fare SR 2 (introduced on an experimental basis, it remains to be seen whether the La Digue buses become a permanent feature).

Timetables vary such a lot from route to route that it's only possible in the space available here to give very general information. As a rule, then, services operate between 5.30 a.m. and 7.00 p.m. during the week (in some cases, however, only at peak times). On many routes there is a considerably reduced service on Saturdays and Sundays; in some cases buses do not run at all. Enquiries are probably best made at your hotel as to what

time the last buses leave Port Glaud, Takamaka, Bel Ombre, etc. for Victoria and/or your hotel itself. Times given will always be approximate – no-one will be willing to be more exact!

Personal impressions of bus travel in the Seychelles are featured in "Highlights" (see p. 41); one or two fares and other details are included in "Useful Information" (see p. 160).

A final point: those who are used to driving on the right-hand side of the road should remember that things are the other way around in the Seychelles. So be sure to wait for the bus on the right side of the road, i.e. the *left-hand* side when looking in the direction you're travelling!

Boat trips in a place like the Seychelles are surely as important – if not more important – than excursion on land.

As always, Mahé offers the widest range of possible tours. To start with, the Ste. Anne Marine National Park lies just off-shore, almost on the doorstep as it were. This marine park comprises the islands of Ste. Anne, Cerf, Moyenne, Cachée, Round Island and Long Island, as well as the coral reefs surrounding them. Round trips in glass-bottomed boats reveal all the splendour and variety of the underwater world between the coral; conditions are ideal for snorkelling. Leading travel agents offer full-day and half-day tours from Victoria to Round Island, Cerf and Moyenne; all tours allow time for swimming and/or snorkelling and full-day tours include a midday meal on Round Island or Moyenne Island. Prices per person for such excursions range between SR 100 and SR 210.

Islands somewhat farther afield can also be visited within the framework of organised excursions from Mahé: for example, Silhouette, North Island, Aride Island, and Praslin/La Digue in combination. Prices here will range between SR 380 and SR 500 per person.

Above and beyond such tours, there is of course the possibility of hiring boats in Victoria. For more details of this, see "Useful Information/Chartering Boats", p.161.

From Praslin it's possible to cross to La Digue by motorized schooner – either the "Lady Mary II" or the "Silhouette". The crossing takes around half an hour (depending on weather conditions); outward journey in the morning, return in the afternoon. Other possibilities include trips to the bird islands of Cousin and Aride or to Curieuse with the marine national park of the same name. Those staying on Praslin should enquire at the hotel reception about departure times, prices and charter boats. Alternatively, keep an eye out for notices detailing excursions, organised by travel agencies.

Island Hopping in the trim aircraft of the Seychelles' own airline is one of the most charming and exhilarating ways of getting to know the islands – simply because the "bird's eye view" adds another dimension. An iridescent sea shimmers in countless shades of blue and green, coral banks are a mass of yellows and browns and greens. Dotted about in the wide expanse of the ocean, the islands appear like splashes of vivid green fringed with sands of the palest gold and encircled by a silvery halo as the waves break on reefs. Reason enough to make sure that at least one airborne excursion features in your itinerary!

There is a choice of day trips (from Mahé) to and from Frégate and Praslin (in both cases the flight takes approx. 15 mins), sometimes combined with a boat trip to Cousin Island or La Digue. "Island Hopping" combinations from Mahé include stopovers on Praslin, La Digue and Bird Island.

If you have planned (and booked) to spend part of your holiday on Bird Island or Denis Island (days which in retrospect may well turn out to be the highlight of your Seychelles experience), your longer "island hop" will, of course, be considered part of your complete travel arrangements (and will be included in that price).

Island combinations are the way to add spice to a Seychelles holiday. While day trips can do much to convey something of the charm of a place, spending a few days on a particular island gives a true impression of that island's very individual character. Of the smaller islands of the Seychelles (i.e. besides Mahé), accommodation is available on Praslin, La Digue, Frégate, Silhouette, Bird Island, Denis Island and Felicité as well as on Moyenne and L'Islette (the latter two islands are not included in tour operators' programmes). A single destination in the Outer Islands has been opened to tourism: Desroches, the largest of the Amirantes islands, is now linked by air and has a lodge where full board is available.

Should you wish to combine Mahé with another of the Seychelles islands, it's best to book accordingly from the outset. It is, of course, possible to make such a booking at a travel agency in Mahé but the necessary cancellation of confirmed booking at a hotel in Mahé could lead to problems with the accounts. In the same way, you may find that if you try to extend your holiday in order to include a stay an another island you'll be prevented from doing so by difficulties in changing your flight home.

Mahé Round Trip

Beau Vallon, an important centre of tourism an Mahé, was chosen as the starting point and final destination of this tour of the island. Should your hotel be located elsewhere, simply join the route there.

1. North Mahé from Beau Vallon to Victoria (via Glacis, North Point and North East Point)

For most of the way to North East Point the coast road is slightly elevated, affording fine views of the rocky coast and the sand beaches strewn be-

tween headlands. Driving north along the west coast, you'll pass the Northolme, Sunset Beach and Vista do Mar hotels (before, in and after Glacis respectively). Along the north coast, the road winds its way between luxurious private villas dotted among the cliffs. There are a number of popular restaurants on the flat and fairly straight stretch of road along the east coast to Victoria.

2. East Coast from Victoria to Anse Royale (via Cascade, the airport and Pointe au Sel)

The east coast road leading to the airport begins at Victoria's southernmost roundabout (access via Francis Rachel St. and 5th June Ave.). After a few hundred metres you'll see the entrance to the Botanical Garden. Almost all the way to the airport, the coast road is lined with buildings: small

Creole house in Beau Vallon

houses and shops but also businesses enterprises such as car dealers' and the Sey Brewery. Just before the airport, the road (particularly narrow at this point) crosses the lagoon of Anse

Talbot on supports built between huge granite boulders.

Beyond the airport, at Pointe La Rue, the road turns due south and then follows the edge of Anse aux Pins, passing plantations (mostly coconut) on the other side. After the Reef Hotel (on the left), look out for the entrance to the "Craft Village" on the right (traditional workshops and stores selling handcrafts as well as the "Pomme Cannelle" restaurant specializing in Seychellois cuisine; the carefully-restored colonial planter's house of the former St. Roch plantation is the pride of the village). Continuing, on the right hand side there are a number of old colonial houses to be discovered (at times impossible without help from locals; houses at various stages of dilapidation). Just beyond Pointe au Sel, crest of the road offers glorious view over Anse Royale Bay with the tiny granite and palm island of Souris and Anse Royale itself. Popular beaches on the calm waters of the lagoon, at first hidden by dense vegetation but then adjoining open coconut groves.

3. South Mahé from Anse Royale to Anse Boileau (via Anse Bougainville, Anse Marie-Louise, Quatre Bornes, Takamaka and Baie Lazare)

Passing the southern part of Anse Royale, Anse Bougainville and Cap Lascars, we reach Anse Marie-Louise. Here, where the road turns inland, it's possible to continue along the coast on a track leading to a footpath – the walk to Anse Capucins and Police Bay is worthwhile. The round trip continues on the Quatre Bornes Rd. heading inland. In Quatre Bornes itself a secondary road leads down to Anse Intendance and Police Bay.

The main road continues to Takamaka, skirts Anse Takamaka and Baie Lazare (on which the Plantation Club Hotel stands), follows the wide sweeping bay of Anse à la Mouche and then carries on to Anse Boileau.

Between Baie Lazare and Anse à la Mouche you could stop off to pay a call on Michael Adams, the painter (see p. 50); there are a number of good restaurants along this southern stretch of the Mahé coast.

4. West Coast from Anse Boileau to Port Glaud (via Grand' Anse).

From Anse Boileau to Grand' Anse, the road (asphalted just a few years ago) either runs along the coast or cuts through plantations. Just before Grand' Anse Village (beach of same name) you'll pass the Mèridien Barbarons Beach Hotel; shortly after that the approach road to the Equator Grand Anse Residence Hotel branches off.

Just short of Port Glaud you'll see the Seychelles Sheraton Hotel on a rocky elevation on the coast and Thérère Island lying off-shore. From Port Glaud access to the smaller island L'Islette.

5. Port Glaud – Sans Souci Rd. – Victoria – Beau Vallon

The Sans Souci Rd. is without doubt the most spectacular road linking east and west coasts of the island. Winding and curving its way through the mountainous interior, the road reaches a maximum elevation of 500 m (1,640 ft). Along this route you'll also pass the largest tea plantations of the Seychelles and a tea factory (tours possible); a number of hiking trails head off into the surrounding mountains from the road.

In Victoria take the first road left after the clock tower (i.e. Revolution Ave.) in order to return to Beau Vallon via the St. Louis pass. Between Victoria and Beau Vallon there are a number of places worthy of a short detour: Le Niol (view across North West Bay as far as Silhouette Island); Bel Ombre (incl. Méridien Fisherman's Cove Hotel); and Danzilles, where the Hotel Auberge Club des Seychelles stands atop a cliff looking out high above the sea. For more details of conditions and facilities for bathing on the beaches of the south, southwest and west coasts

of Mahé, see the chapter "ABC of the Islands and Beaches", p.70).

For the drive form the west to the east coast (5th stage of the trip), it's also possible to opt at Grand' Anse for the La Misère Rd. Like the Sans Souci Rd., it offers wonderful views of the west coast and in addition boasts a panoramic view of the east coast including Cerf Island and Ile Cachée.

For the purposes of further tours, there are another two roads that cross the island from east to west, this time further south: the Montagne Posée Rd. between Anse aux Pins and Anse Boileau (relatively quiet road) and Les Canelles Rd. between Anse Royale and Anse à la Mouche (south Mahé's most important traverse). The third possibility to cross the island in the south, the Quatre Bornes Rd., was described on the third leg of the round trip.

What's that in Creole?

The Seychelles have three "national" languages, a fact that will become apparent at the very latest when you open the government newspaper *Nation*: some articles will be in English, others in French and a number will be in Creole.

The theory that you'll always be able to get by with English is only really true of encounters with Seychellois who are actively involved in tourism, i.e. staff of hotels and travel agencies, taxi drivers (for the most part). By no means all the local people will un-

derstand a question put to them in English. So for those who intend to "go it alone" on the islands, moving around fairly independently, a few words of Creole will be very useful.

If you can speak French you should have no major problems getting the hang of Creole. As in other places where the French influence is, or has been, considerable (e. g. Mauritius, Martinique, New Orleans), the Creole of the Seychelles contains very many features of the language (this will be clear if you compare some of the phrases listed below – in English, Creole and French. Unstressed syllables in a French word are contracted, and soft sounds are often transformed into hard sounds. For example, "chaise" (chair) becomes "sez" in Creole.

As far as pronunciation is concerned, take care to pronounce every syllable in Creole.

Conversation Openers

Good morning.	Bonzour.	Bonjour.
Good night.	Bonswar.	Bonsoir.
Goodbye.	Orevwar.	Au revoir.
How are you?	Koman sava?	Comment ça va?
I'm fine thank you.	Mon byen, mersi.	Très bien, merci.
What's your name?	Koman ou apele?	Comment vous appelez-vous?
My name is George.	Mon apel George.	Je m'appelle George.
Are you French?	Ou Franse?	Vous êtes français?
Swiss?	Swiss?	Suisse?
German? Seychellois?	Alman? Seselwa?	Allemand? Seychellois?
No, I'm English.	Non mon Angle.	Non, je suis anglais.

Out and About

What time does the plane leave, please?	Keler avyon i kite, silvouple?	A quelle heure est-ce que l'avion part, s'il vous plaît?
Is it far?	I lwen?	C'est loin?
Is it near?	I pre?	C'est près?
Is this our coach?	Sa nou bis? Nou bis sa?	C'est notre bus?
Is this our boat?	Sa nou bato? Nou bato sa?	C'est notre bateau?
Are we going to Victoria?	Nou pe al Victoria?	Nous partons à Victoria?
Are you going to Praslin?	Ou pe al Praslin?	Vous partez à Praslin?
Yes, we are going to Victoria.	Wi, nou pe al Victoria.	Oui, nous partons à Victoria.
No, I'm not going to Praslin.	Non, mon pa pe al Praslin	Non, je ne pars pas à Praslin.

Questions

Where is...please?	Oli...silvouple?	Où est...s'il vous plaît?
the bank	labank	la banque
the market	bazar	le marché le bazar
the bar	bar	le bar
my room	mon lasanm	ma chambre
my luggage	mon bagaz	mes bagages
my key	mon lakle (laclay)	ma clef

English	Seychellois	French
Where are we now?	Kote nou ete la?	Où sommes-nous maintenant?
Where do you live?	Kote ou reste?	Où habitez-vous?

Shopping, Eating Out

English	Seychellois	French
How much is this?	Konbyen sa?	Combien coûte?
How much is this...? (shell)?	Konbyen sa...? (kokiy)?	Combien coûte (cette coquille)?
How much do I owe you?	Konbyen mon dwa ou?	Combien je vous dois?
This is beautiful.	Sa i zoli.	C'est joli.
One of this (these), please.	En sa, silvouple.	J'en prends un, s'il vous plaît.
It's not very good.	Pa tro bon.	Ce n'est pas très bon.
Can I have a beer please?	Mon kapa ganny en labyer silvouple?	Une bière, s'il vous plaît.
Would you like to dance?	Oule danse?	Voulez-vous danser?
Can you do the séga?	Ou kapa danse séga?	Vous savez danser séga?
Yes I can. How about you?	Wi mon kapa. Be ou?	Oui, je le sais. Et vous?
Let us dance this séga.	Annou danse sa séga.	Allons danser cette séga.
Would you like a drink?	Ouele en bwar?	Voulez-vous quelque chose à boire?
The menu, please.	Meni, silvouple.	La carte, s'il vous plaît.
The bill (check), please.	Bil, silvouple.	L'addition, s'il vous plaît.
That's for you.	Sa pou ou.	C'est pour vous.
What time does the bar close?	Keler bar i fermen?	A quelle heure ferme le bar?
I'm tired.	Mon fatige (fa-ti-gay).	Je suis fatigué.
I'm going to bed.	Mon pe al dormi.	Je m'en vais me coucher.

Useful Phrases

English	Seychellois	French
Excuse me, can I have a light please?	Eskiz mwan, ou annan dife silvouple?	Excusez-moi. Avez-vous du feu, s'il vous plaît?
What is the time, please?	Keler i ete silvouple?	Quelle heure est-il?
What is the date today?	Ki dat ozordi?	Quelle est la date aujourd'hui?
This beach is beautiful.	Sa lans i zoli.	Cette plage est jolie. (anse is the Seychellois term for beach/bay)
What is this beach called?	Komanyer sa lans i apele?	Comment s'appelle cette plage?
What is this fish called?	Komanyer sa pwason i apele?	Comment s'appelle ce poisson?
The Seychelles are very beautiful.	Sesel i byen zoli.	Les Seychelles sont très jolies.
Many thanks.	Mersi bokou.	Merci beaucoup.
this morning	osordi, bomaten	aujourd'hui, ce matin
tomorrow	demen	demain
the day after tomorrow	apredmen	après-demain
yesterday	yer	hier

Sports in the Seychelles

run for beginners. On the beach at Beau Vallon Bay (Mahé) there are a number of schools which are not attached to a particular hotel. The Beau Vallon Watersports Centre and the Seychelles Windsurfing Limited are affiliated with international windsurfing associations.

In order to avoid getting thrown off continually – not to mention having to forgo one's pleasure completely because of strong winds and choppy waters – it's as well to bear the following in mind: for the duration of the southeast monsoon (May to October), opt for the leeward side of the islands (in the case of Mahé the northwest and west coasts); in the period of the northwest monsoon (November to April), best conditions will be found on the east coast of Mahé (where the choice of hotels is, however, more limited than around either Beau Vallon Bay or Grand' Anse).

Water Sports
The thing about islands is that they're surrounded by water... and therefore offer the best possible conditions for water sports of all kinds. The Seychelles are no exception. The range of sports available does, however, vary considerably from island to island and does depend upon the location of a particular hotel.

Windsurfing has over the years become a very popular sport in the Seychelles. Hotels on Mahé, Praslin and Denis Island include it in their programmes of activities, and not only for experienced surfers: courses are also

Sailing, as another "wind sport", is subject to the same conditions as windsurfing. Appropriate facilities are offered by hotels on the northwest and east coasts of Mahé and on the west and east coasts of Praslin. Yachts and sailing boats are available for hire (by the hour or day) from the Yacht Club in Victoria; limited membership (for the duration of your stay) can be arranged.

Waterskiing requires waters which are particularly calm and not too shallow. This being the case, conditions are best from May to October (i.e. at the time of the southeast monsoon) in Beau Vallon Bay. This doesn't mean, however, that there's no waterskiing between November and April; providing the wind drops, a round on skis will be possible (equipment from the Beau Vallon Watersports Centre).

Paragliding (or parasailing) dominates the scene on sunny days at Beau Vallon Bay. Sometimes you'll see several colourful parachutes being towed through the air by speedboats. Gliding over the surface of the water, one's legs dangling in the air, paragliding is more a pleasure than a sport. Its popularity is increasing all the time. Conditions, seasonal variations, etc., as for waterskiing.

Snorkelling is particularly worthwhile in the Seychelles: as a result of strict conservation laws enforced by the government, the underwater world of the islands has been afforded an important measure of protection. The coastal waters appear as a richly-stocked aquarium, the surrounding reefs constituting its outer limits. Above all, the Ste. Anne Marine National Park (see map p. 153) – the marine park on Victoria's "doorstep" – ensures ideal snorkelling all year round. At times of the year when waters are calmer (dictated in the first instance by the monsoons), excellent snorkelling is also possible in other areas: along the coasts of Silhouette and Curieuse, for example, in the marine national parks of the same names (see also "The Seychelles and Conservation", p. 152); in mostly smaller bays along the west and south coasts of Mahé as well as off Praslin, La Digue, Frégate, Bird Island and Denis Island. Now that it's much easier to visit Desroches, the beautiful and manifold snorkelling grounds off that island have also been made accessible to enthusiasts.

For the latest information on facilities, water conditions, etc. inquire at your hotel or at a local travel agency. Alternatively, apply to a diving centre (if there is one in your vicinity). The diving centres on the islands are also the places to inquire about snorkelling excursions.

Snorkelling can be enjoyed by anyone who can swim. The buoyancy of the salt water is such that one really has to do nothing at all to stay on the surface of the water – save perhaps a gentle kick of one's flippers from time to time. Flippers, mask and the snorkel itself are all the equipment you'll need. Relatively inexpensive, they are sometimes known as the "ABC of diving gear" for water sports fans. Those who don't bring along their own from home can either buy them from sports shops on Mahé or hire them – hotels sometimes have equipment for hire, otherwise from diving clubs.

When snorkelling it's important to bear in mind that exposure to the sun at the surface of the water is of greater intensity than when lying on the beach. Guard against sunburn by applying suntan oil generously before entering the water and by wearing a T-shirt while swimming. As always, beware in particular of the intense midday sun; far less chance of being burnt in the mornings and afternoons.

More than 300 species of fish and over 100 species of coral are to be found in the reefs and shallow waters of the Seychelles. Snorkelling allows one the perfect opportunity to marvel at the wealth of underwater wildlife. Fish, coral, molluscs... all are protected in the Seychelles and regulations are strictly enforced. Spear fishing is prohibited and punishments for offenders are severe. While on the subject, taking a spear gun along as a precautionary measure is totally unnecessary in Seychelles waters. No shark attack on swimmers, snorkellers or divers has ever been reported in the area. While there are shark species here, they are small (up to approx. 1 m/just over 3 ft in length) and present no threat to humans.

Scuba diving will turn one's encounter with the underwater world of the Seychelles into a (literally!) profounder experience. The enchanting glimpses afforded by snorkelling will turn into a throughgoing exploration of its greater depths as one scuba dives. Which is not to say that divers always automatically descend to considerable depths – equally fascinating are the natural colours of the underwater world just beneath the surface of the water.

Those who need to learn the basic skills of diving should apply to a diving school such as that of the Seychelles Underwater Centre at the Coral Strand Hotel (Beau Vallon Bay, Mahé). Courses (of several days duration) cover the theoretical side of diving and familiarize prospective divers with the use of the breathing apparatus. Prerequisites include a minimum age of 16 years, a medical attest of physical fitness and preferably experience in swimming and snorkelling.

For experienced and licensed divers, the Underwater Centre runs advanced courses along PADI guide-lines, e.g.

advanced open water courses and underwater photography courses.

For a list of the diving schools and/or bases on Mahé, Praslin and La Digue, see "Useful Information" p.162.

In the vicinity of the granite islands (primarily the waters around Mahé, Silhouette, Praslin and La Digue) there are more than twenty interesting diving sites. Added to this come the grounds near Bird Island, Denis Island and the Outer Islands. Underwater conditions vary according to the season of the year (or, to be more precise, according to the monsoons). Generally-speaking, however, the most favourable period is from April to November, when those diving grounds which are least affected by the southeast monsoon (and that means the majority) offer ideal diving conditions. What's more, this period encompasses the several calm days which occur when one monsoon season gives way to another (April/May and October/November). But from December to March, too, divers will find excellent sport in the Seychelles – if, that is, they head for grounds which are shielded from the main force of the northwest monsoon (this is the case off the east and south coasts of Mahé and in the Ste. Anne Marine National Park; sheltered on all sides, the latter represents a year-round destination for diving enthusiasts).

Visibility at depth (which never falls under 20 m/66 ft) can be as much as 50 metres and more (around 165 ft) on absolutely calm days. Dangerous currents rarely occur, even in narrower channels.

Deep-sea fishing is becoming an ever more important sporting activity in the Seychelles. Reports of catches to date speak of blue and black marlin, tuna, wahoos, barracuda and bonitos...

The Seychelles can also lay claim to being one of the three regions where dogtooth tuna *(Gymnosarda unicolor)* is caught. Since this tunny was officially declared a game fish by the IGFA (International Game Fish Association) in 1975, Denis Island alone has been able to break the world record on five separate occasions.

The waters around the coral islands of Bird and Denis, while prized for their wealth of both small and large game fish (bonefish, marlin, spearfish, etc.), are still largely "unknown territory". Thanks to their location at the edge of the Seychelles Bank, however, one might be forgiven for thinking that they were created for the purposes of game fishing. For, while the depth of water over the Seychelles Bank itself reaches a maximum of just 70 m (230 ft), the sea bed drops away abruptly at its edge, creating depths of

some 1,800 m (almost 6,000 ft). Which means that while the granite islands (grouped in the middle of the bank) enjoy the benefit associated with shallower waters, the likes of Bird and Denis Island have the advantages of greater depth. The waters here are, for example, eminently suited to the traditional fishing methods of the islanders – line and sinker. The usual catch includes resplendently colourful fish with Creole names which are just as colourful: *bourgeois, varavara, Dame Berry* and *Capitaine Rouge*.

Deep-sea fishing excursions can be booked in Mahé (the best place to do so is the Seychelles Marine Charter Association in Victoria, where it's also possible to book to join a fishing party and thereby divide charter costs). Those staying on Praslin, La Digue, Bird Island and Denis Island will find that a number of hotels also arrange for fishing excursions. Hotels mostly have their own boats, the latter fitted out for deep-sea fishing. (See also "Useful Information/Chartering Boats", p.161.)

Fishing tackle is available for hire but supplies are very limited, so it is

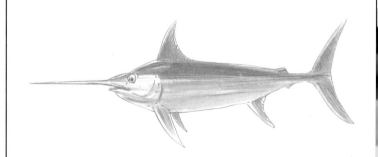

recommended that people bring their own from home.

The period from November to April is considered the best time for deep-sea fishing. July and August, while also favourable, are less suitable since the southeast monsoon can mean that the sea becomes very choppy.

Sports on Dry Land

While it would be impossible to match the ideal conditions and excellent facilities for water sports, around the Seychelles it is possible to partake in a number of sporting activities on the islands themselves – as ever, Mahé offers the widest choice.

Tennis facilities can be found in hotels on the northwest, west and east coasts; some courts are equipped with floodlighting. The modern "Tartan Court" of the Equator Residence Hotel and the three hard courts at the Méridien Fisherman's Cove Hotel should meet the demands of more exacting players. Luckily, tennis facilities on the islands are being extended and improved all the time. This being the case, it's probably best to rely on tour operators' catalogues for up-to-date information on hotels with courts.

Golf on the islands is concentrated upon the 9-hole course at the Reef Hottel Golf Club (on the east coast of Mahé). Hotel guests pay no green fees; non-residents are required to take out temporary membership of the club.

Cycling is most popular on Praslin and La Digue. Tours on Praslin can be quite strenuous thanks to the many steep stretches of road leading to and from the Vallée de Mai; racing downhill after the steady climb is often quite a thrilling experience! Rates of hire for bicycles are unfortunately rather high (see Useful Information/Bicycle Hire, p.160).

Hiking is perhaps a surprising sporting activity to find on the Seychelles. It may well be more accurate to talk of extended walks... then again, trails do lead into the mountainous interior of Mahé and require sturdy shoes.

The Victoria Trail is, as its name suggests, a circuit through and around the capital.

"Trois Frères" is the name given to a trail heading out from Sans Souci (2 km south of Victoria) and taking in any number of rare trees and other plants and, providing the weather is clear, affording fine views of the outlying islands. Trail takes approx. 3 hours.

The Anse Major Trail starts out from Danzilles (B1) and takes one through the northwest of Mahé; here, too, there are many fascinating flowers, shrubs and trees to see along the way.

For more details (including information on walks with an experienced local guide), apply to the Tourist Information office in Independence House, Victoria.

Other sports such as squash, badminton, mini golf, table tennis, croquet and bocce often feature on the programme of leisure pursuits offered by hotels. The Seychelles College also welcomes guest players.

Souvenirs

Your first Seychelles souvenir should be bought as soon as possible after your arrival as it will serve you well for the duration of your stay. The wide-brimmed hats skilfully woven out of palm or banana leaves – and worn by many Seychellois men and women – shield head and neck from the intense, almost perpendicular rays of the equatorial sun. Far more effective protection than any suntan oil can offer.

Together with baskets and table mats (also made of the same versatile material), these hats are probably the lightest items you could choose to take home as a souvenir. Other items which won't weigh too heavily on the airport scales include batik or hand printed fabric (both worked into light and airy beachwear, cheery T-shirts and colourful *pareos*) and coral or mother-of-pearl jewellery. Finely-worked and very varied in style, pieces of coral and mother-of-pearl jewellery will be found in "better class" shops and boutiques: for example, in the Victoria Arcades, in the Pirates Arms Building, in Beau Vallon, Bel Ombre and Anse à la Mouche, as well as in most hotel boutiques.

Tiny rag dolls in typical Seychelles dress are also hardly likely to make an impression on your luggage allowance on the way home. The same is true of the necklaces worn by many a Seychelloise and consisting of strings of red and black seeds attractively alternating with white sharks' teeth. The effect is most appealing, more than can be said for the sharks' jaws which you may well find bared on souvenir stalls, for

example at the market. White walking sticks fashioned from the backbone of a whale are almost certain to catch your eye; you'll usually find them among the store of items offered by souvenir sellers on Victoria's Independence Avenue, between the Pirates Arms Café and the Clock Tower. The white coral and selection of shells you'll also find there certainly appear less gruesome than the whale bones, but one should bear in mind that our enjoyment of every piece of intricate coral and every beautiful shell has meant plundering the reefs and despoiling Nature. To refrain from buying is to add force to the age-old rule of the marketplace: falling demand means that supply becomes superfluous.

Perhaps you'll find something that appeals to you among the stands at the corner by the Clock Tower; there you'll find any number of crafted articles made of wood, shells, coconuts, palm straw, etc. You may well be very tempted by the tortoiseshell pieces – whether a bracelet or salad servers, all are without a doubt very decorative. Beware of falling for such attractive offers, however. The tortoiseshell used stems from the hawksbill turtle or the loggerhead turtle, both of which are protected by CITES, the Convention on International Trade in Endangered Species. The aim of this international agreement is the eradication of all trade in species which are threatened with extinction as a result of exploitation at the hand of man. Great Britain, the United States, Canada, Australia and New Zealand are all signatory states of the CITES agreement. Any items banned by the agreement (and this includes the above-mentioned tortoiseshell) will automatically be confiscated by the customs authorities in signatory states. The fact that trade in tortoiseshell is still legal in the Seychelles in no way affects this policy. So, in order to avoid unnecessary vexation at customs, do refrain from buying this kind of souvenir. In so doing you will also be making an important contribution to the protection of endangered species.

Charming souvenirs – the work of local craftsmen – can be obtained in Mahé's "Craft Village" (opened 1988), which is located on the east coast road near the Reef Hotel (Anse aux Pins.). The same type of gifts can be purchased in the "Seypot" in Les Mamelles; this cooperative produces truly tasteful ceramics and offers the same for sale directly to the public.

In order to recall the tastes of the Seychelles – or to share those tastes with friends at home – one might opt for a sachet or two of spices. These can be bought in the Indian stores around the market, or on the market itself.

Tea is another good idea and is easily obtainable in shops in Victoria or directly from the "Tea Tavern" on the Sans Souci Road. Alternatively, you could wait until your departure and take advantage of the stocks of tea at the duty-free shop at the airport – one possible way of using up those remaining rupees. For those emptying pockets and purces in this way, the reasonably-priced 50-gramme packets are a very good idea (250-gramme packs are also available, of course).

Otherwise, the choice of goods on offer in the duty-free shop is rather limited. One finds the usual range of international brands of cigarettes and spirits; there are no real bargains to be had.

Two further souvenir ideas typical of the Seychelles (one in fact unique to the islands) require a little more care in the purchasing.

Firstly, there are stamps – a large selection of truly beautiful Seychelles stamps is available at the philatelic counter of Victoria's main post office. At a neighbouring counter interesting first-day covers may be purchased. Some single covers date from a period ten or fifteen years ago and are sold today for only a little more than their face value at the time of issue, which means there are quite a few bargains to be had.

And then there is the coco-de-mer. Unique to the Seychelles and probably the most sought-after of souvenirs, your coco-de-mer will cost you rather more than any other of the items mentioned but does represent a notable investment – after all, Nature did show as much imagination in the formation of the two-lobed nut of the palm as she did when she created Eve. Whether to opt for the whole nut (in its natural state or highly polished) or choose instead an object fashioned from it – vases, fruit dishes, salad bowls – will very much depend upon your luggage situation and your budget. It's as well to be aware that a number of very convincing imitation coco-de-mer nuts are also offered for sale on the islands. Such "mini versions" (they are about the size of a man's fist) may well catch your eye at the stalls opposite the post office in Victoria, or in any number of other places. What you're looking for are replicas fashioned in burnished wood and complete with coconut fibris attached at the vital spots.

While on the subject of replicas, models of fishing boats and historical sailing ships are sold in the "La Marine" workshops. The quality of these handcrafted pieces is excellent; as one would expect, they are not exactly inexpensive. It's possible that you won't find the business premises of the "La Marine" in their rightful place, i.e. in La Cap on Mahés East Coast Road. The beautiful old colonial house which contains the workshops is in line for restoration (middle 1988) and so the workshops may well have been moved temporarily to the nearby Craft Village. Transporting larger model ships by air (in sturdy packing cases) should present no problems on scheduled flights, when they will be considered normal luggage or perhaps excess luggage. Be prepared to pay an import tax (for ornamental pieces in wood) on arrival home.

Those looking for an even more prestigious souvenir might wander along to the Galerie d'Art N.1 (State House Avenue, Mahé Trading Building, Victoria) or to Christy's Art Gallery (Quincy Street, Victoria). Both galleries exhibit the work of artists living and working in the Seychelles (whether they be locals or people who have chosen to settle on the islands).

You'll find watercolours, graphic arts, batik pieces – all most individual in style. If you're lucky enough to find the galleries open, you'll also be able to obtain the addresses of the individual artists. Most will be happy to receive visitors in their studios. If you chance upon an artist whose work appeals to you, you may still be able to raise quite a treasure in the Seychelles!

And finally, a suggestion for a very personal and inexpensive souvenir of the Seychelles. Why not collect a little bit of sand from the most beautiful beaches you have visited – finer and paler sands are to be found in scarcely another place on earth.

Works of Art in Miniature

Mention stamps from the islands of the Indian Ocean and most people will automatically think of what is arguably philately's greatest historical rarity, the Blue Mauritius. The Seychelles – and indeed most countries the world over – can do little to match such a philatelic celebrity. And how could they be expected to? It was the year 1840 that saw the appearance in London of the first gummed stamp, the famous Penny Black; just a short time later, in

1847, that "unfortunate" misprint occurred in Mauritius, when a stamp was issued bearing the words "Post Office" instead of "Post Paid". The Seychelles had no part to play in those early days of philatelic history since they were still administratively part of Mauritius at the time and issued no stamps of their own.

This deficiency was remedied in 1890 and since then the stamps of the Seychelles have been very popular and

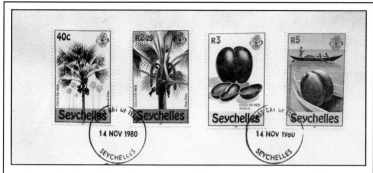

much sought-after collector's items. Particularly the older issues are in demand since their rarity inevitably increases their value. And they are rare: at the turn of the century the population of the Seychelles was still small and postage to foreign destinations amounted to no more than a handful of letters two or three times a month (depending on the more or less regular departures of ships for foreign parts). All of which means that when Seychellois stamps are auctioned abroad nowadays (especially in London), dealers and collectors are always ready for an exciting bidding session... and sellers expect a tidy profit!

More recent issues of Seychelles stamps do not, of course, bring such prices but are still very worthwhile buys. Any international "beauty contest" judged on choice of motif, artistic presentation and technical skill in engraving and printing would be the richer for its contestants from the Seychelles, and the latter would have more than a good chance of bringing in the prizes.

A collection of the stamps which have been issued in the last fifteen years resembles an extensive, exotic picture book through the Seychelles.

There are giant tortoises and chameleons, impressive coco-de-mer palms and wild vanilla; there are oxcarts and trucks which function as public buses, schooners and royal yachts (on the occasion of the marriage of Prince Charles and Lady Diana). Wading ibises and fluttering fairy terns adorn other stamps; wild flowers and orchids bloom, marine tortoises and coral fish swim about; and even the opening of scheduled services by the Air Seychelles warranted the issue of a special (and very attractive) stamp by the postal authorities.

To "tell the people what Seychelles are" is the guiding principle of the postal authorities. In a wise move they limit new issues to five per year. The success of their policy can be seen in the fact that the beautiful postage stamps of the islands now earn as much for their homeland as does the ever popular coconut, not to mention cinnamon and a number of other products.

Use them as they were intended and the stamps add a colourful and charming finishing touch to your postcards home. Alternatively, you could purchase a selection and keep them as souvenirs in their own right.

Photo Tips

Getting your photographic equipment together for a trip to the Seychelles requires no more preparation than it would for a trip elsewhere. So, it is a matter of a routine check that equipment is in working order and that batteries are still functioning. Nothing more disappointing than wonderful shots that don't come out for one reason or another, so if in any doubt, ask your dealer. It's also as well to bear in mind that batteries which have been in use for a longer period of time can "die" when suddenly asked to meet the requirements of the newly-arrived (and very enthusiastic) photographer – remember to take along some spares.

In view of the strong lighting conditions in the Seychelles, your supply of film should be primarily composed of slow to medium-fast emulsions such as 25 ASA/ISO or 64 ASA/ISO. If, however, you intend to go to the Valée de Mai, the site on Praslin where the coco-de-mer is found, you will be better off with somewhat faster film (e.g. 200 ASA/ISO or even 400 ASA/ISO). This will enable you to take photographs under the thick canopy of leaves, which might otherwise not be possible. This would be especially advantageous if you have the great fortune of lining up a Seychelles black parrot with your telephoto or zoom lens.

Taking photographs in the intense light of the midday sun mostly brings disappointing results. Being very near the equator, you'll find that the sun at midday beats down from directly above, making portraits, for example, problematic – even the very slight projection of the brow casts a consider-

able shadow and often means that eyes appear as two dark holes. One ingenious solution to this problem is to use a small flash – not a question of the kind of illumination needed for indoor photography, but of boosting the light in insufficiently lit areas. Recommending the use of a built in flash is not something that can be done without a word of caution: this kind of flash is usually calibrated for a distance of between 3 m and 5 m (between approx. 10 ft and 16 ft) and may well "overshoot" the portrait range of 1-2 m (approx. 3-6 ft). One might try remedying this by placing a white cloth (e.g. a handkerchief) over the flash, thus lessening its intensity.

The bright midday sun can also mean that care is needed when taking beach shots. The strong sunlight reflected by large expanses of light sand easily misleads the light meter. A false reading – one registering more light than is in fact the case – will result in an incorrect f-stop, insufficient exposure, and photos in which people, palms and decorative granite cliffs (i.e. the actual subjects of your picture) are too dark. Adjusting readings to suit people, palms and granite cliffs will mean correct exposure for these parts of the photograph but will produce sand that is as white as the driven snow.

The long and the short of this rather lengthy treatise: you'd be well recommended to leave such "bathed-in-sunshine" shots well alone between 11 a.m. and 2 p.m. (to be absolutely sure, even add an hour either side). Professionals working on the Seychelles limit their photo sessions to the period between 7.30 a.m. and 10 a.m. and again between 3.30 p.m. and 6 p.m., when light conditions are optimum. Keep to these times and you're sure to have more joy with your pictures... and less wasted film!

Heat has to be one of the worst enemies of film, be it unexposed or exposed. Which is not to say that film will be ruined just as soon as ever it feels the heat of the tropics. Still, one should try to ensure that film is exposed to heat for as short a period of time as possible. So, for example, if you're heading off on an excursion, don't take all your supply with you but instead only as much as you'll need for that particular trip. Make a point of removing exposed films from your bag as soon as you return to your hotel; keep them in a cool place along with unused films (your hotel room will presumably be air-conditioned, so this should not be a problem). Placing films in a plastic bag helps to protect them from excess humidity.

A plastic bag can also help to protect cameras from two more archenemies: sand and sea water. If sand should get into your camera, clean thoroughly with a fine, soft brush; use a soft cloth to wipe off splashes of salt water. If the "splashes" were in fact a thorough soaking, even total immersion, you may be lucky and find that drying – for example, with a hair dryer – restores the camera to working order. But don't let that fool you: the salt will continue to eat away surreptitiously at both mechanical and electronic parts. There's only one thing for it – make sure you get the camera to the maker's maintenance and repair department as soon as possible after your return home. If there's anything

to be done, they're in the best position to do it.

Underwater colour photography is a discipline unto itself. The deeper you go, the more colours (all except blue) are filtered out by the water. Which means that a flash is an essential part of your equipment if you're to capture the true range of colours of the underwater world. Working without a flash in Seychelles waters, it is usually possible to photograph up to a depth of about 3 m (10 ft). – the waters are particularly clear around Mahé, Praslin, La Digue; such photos do much to convey the atmosphere of the deep. But if you want to catch the fascinating colours of the fish living amid the coral, then even nearer the surface you have to resort to flash.

Out of the water and into the air... and first of all a tip for those using fully automatic cameras (i.e. those which also focus automatically). One often hears disappointed tales of how photos taken with such cameras from the inside of an aircraft didn't come out. How could they be expected to: light reflected from the window of the plane means that the camera can not focus accurately on the desired object beyond. Remedy this by holding the camera right up against the window pane. Either that or photograph out at an angle of around 20° (there may be slight variations here; see the operating instructions which accompanied your camera).

The Seychellois are not unhappy to find themselves the object of photographers' interest. On the other hand, they don't take kindly to being caught unawares: so, make a point of asking permission first. An enquiring glance, a nod of the head, a friendly gesture with the camera is usually all it takes to reach an understanding. If people react by shaking their heads or turning away, their reluctance should of course be respected and no further attempts made to persuade. It's a pleasure to find that the ring of coins still has no part in such exchanges, be it as a show of appreciation on the part of the photographer or as a kind of fee claimed by his "model". You may even find that offering money causes a deal of offence. Which is not to say that children won't be delighted with a few sweets, adults with the chance to try a foreign brand of cigarette or a mini flacon of perfume.

Another tip on the technical side: darker skins against a light background (sky, sand, pale headgear) can pose problems for the exposure meter; the lighter the background, the more inaccurate the reading is likely to be. This being the case, open your aperture to 5.6 or 4 instead of, say, 8. Automatic cameras will usually have a facility enabling the correction of readings in such a case. Otherwise you might try altering temporarily the indicated film speed (for example, 25 ASA/15 DIN instead of 64 ASA/ 19 DIN). To be on the safe side, repeat "special" shots, with various exposures.

Should you begin to run short of film in the Seychelles, you'll have no problem replenishing your supply; you'll find, however, that prices are quite a lot higher than for the same products at home. The usual range of international brands and popular sizes will be easily available, at least in either of the two photo shops in Victoria (Kim Noon, Kingsgate House, Tel: 22966 and Market Street, Tel: 22252; Photo Eden, Pirates Arms Bldg., Independence Avenue, Tel: 22457). Apply to same for minor repair jobs. Hotel shops will usually stock ample supplies of the most popular films.

As far as developing film is concerned, there are a number of businesses which will accept negative films (both colour and black and white) for developing and printing. There is no service for the developing of slide films, irrespective of the maker.

The Seychelles and Conservation

The tiny land in the endless expanse of the Indian Ocean can well be proud of its record in environmental affairs. For, seen in relation to the size of this island state, the Seychellois have done more to protect the environment than anyone else in the world: around 40 % of their already limited Lebensraum has been given over to national parks and nature reserves.

The Seychelles' commitment to the preservation of their environment – acclaimed in some quarters, vehemently contested in others – began with the fierce battle for the Aldabra islands; the atolls of the Aldabra group surround what is the largest tropical lagoon in the world and provide a last refuge for 150,000 giant tortoises. The struggle ended in 1967 when all plans to use the area for military purposes were thwarted and the "Seychelles Island Foundation" (SIF) was formed under the patronage of the Seychelles' president Albert René.

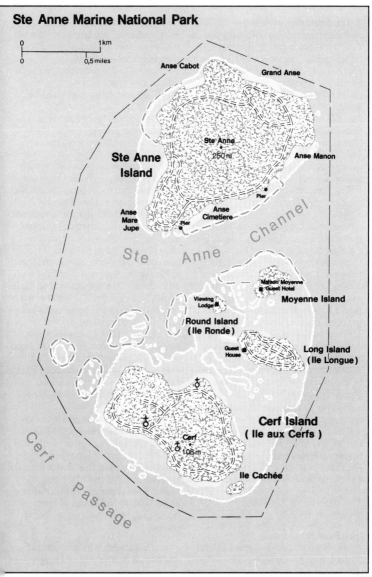

Ste Anne Marine National Park

0 ——————— 1 km
0 ——————— 0,5 miles

Anse Cabot

Grand Anse

Ste Anne
250 m

**Ste Anne
Island**

Anse Manon

Anse
Mare
Jupe

Pier

Anse
Cimetiere

Pier

Ste   Anne   Channel

Maison Moyenne
Guest Hotel

Moyenne Island

Viewing
Lodge

**Round Island
(Ile Ronde)**

Guest
House

**Long Island
(Ile Longue)**

**Cerf Island
(Ile aux Cerfs)**

Cerf
108 m

Ile Cachée

Cerf

Passage

The Seychelles were one of the first nations of the world to declare a part of their territorial waters a "marine national park". That was in 1973 as the Ste. Anne Marine National Park came into being. Located very near to Victoria (Ste. Anne lies just 6 km/less than 4 miles offshore), the park has an invaluable role to play in ensuring the continued survival of the fascinating (and, thanks to its existence, intact) marine flora and fauna of the region. To visit the park is to enjoy a unique and breathtaking glimpse of nature.

The same objectives lay behind the creation of a number of other protected areas along the Seychelles coast-line: for example, the Port Launay Marine National Park and the Baie Ternay Special Reserve (both in West Mahé). The Curieuse Marine National Park encompasses not only Curieuse Island, its coastal waters and reefs, but also the whole of Curieuse Bay, the territory of the park extending southwards as far as the north coast of Praslin. The year 1988 saw another important step towards the protection of Seychelles' shoreline, waters and reefs from disastrous intervention at the hand of man: namely, the proclamation of the Silhouette Marine National Park.

In order to safeguard the environment in all these parks for future generations – and wishing to ensure that visitors find unadulterated pleasure in the wonders of nature – the Seychelles National Environment Commission has issued the following regulations:

✦ Water sports which in any way endanger the environment are prohibited (this includes high-speed waterskiing, speedboat rides, etc.).
✦ No form of life, no natural habitat thereof, may be damaged in any way, removed or disturbed.
✦ Pollution of any kind is strictly prohibited (visitors are requested to leave no rubbish behind them).
✦ No-one in the park may be in possession of a spear gun.
✦ When anchoring, care must be taken that no coral is damaged.

Experience so far has shown a general willingness to observe these regulations and is said to be encouraging.

Conservation measures undertaken by the Seychelles have also been successful within a wider geographical and ecological sphere. They joined in the petitioning that urged the International Whaling Commission to call a halt to whaling. In addition, the Seychelles have placed whales, dolphins, dugongs (sea cows) and marine turtles under protection within the bounds of their economic zone (200 sea miles around the islands). Spear fishing is prohibited not only in the marine national parks but also in all Seychelles waters.

The birds of the islands enjoy the same degree of protection. Regulations protecting the birds themselves and their habitat are strictly enforced on Frégate Island, Praslin and La Digue, as well as in the two best-known island reserves, Aride and Cousin.

It only remains to mention the renowned national parks of the islands' interiors, where protection is afforded to the unique flora of the Seychelles. Take, for example, the Morne Seychellois National Park on Mahé with its multitude of endemic plants, or Praslin's Vallée de Mai National Park, home of the inimitable coco-de-mer palm.

The Seychelles – truly a world of wonders, a Noah's Ark of Nature.

Seychelles

The following denominations are currently in use:

Notes: Rupees   10, 25, 50, 100

Coins: Cents   1, 5, 10, 25
        Rupees   1, 5

Useful Information

Currency

The standard monetary unit of the Seychelles is the rupee, which is divided into 100 cents.

For the present rate of exchange, see fold-out map at the back of the guide.

Currency Regulations

No limit is placed on the amount of local currency which may be imported or exported. However, few foreign banks carry Seychelles rupees and, if they do, rates of exchange are poor. It is therefore advisable to exchange foreign currency in the Seychelles. There are no restrictions upon the import or export of foreign currencies. It is recommended that larger amounts be declared; export is limited to the amount which was originally imported.

Exchange Facilities

Changing money presents no problems since both banks and hotels offer services; banks offer the better rate of exchange. Since some international flights inevitably arrive outside normal banking hours, passengers are advised to take advantage of the exchange counters at the airport in order to cover initial expenses. These counters open to coincide with each arrival and departure and are your last chance to change back unused rupees before leaving the Seychelles.

Exchange rates offered by banks must correspond with those fixed by the government (these appear daily in the newspaper *Nation*).

Traveller's Cheques, Eurocheques, Credit Cards

Banks and hotels accept traveller's cheques made out in US dollars or any freely convertible currency. Once again, banks offer a better rate of exchange. Only certain shops and restaurants will be willing to accept traveller's cheques in payment. The use of credit cards (in particular, American Express, Diner's Club and Visa) has become quite the norm in hotels with an international clientele; the various car hire firms will also usually accept cards in payment.

Eurocheques made out in pound sterling may be cashed upon presentation of a cheque card in a number of banks on Mahé but not on the smaller islands.

Entry Formalities

A valid passport is required in order to enter the Seychelles. On arrival, visitors are issued with a visa which is valid for 30 days. This visa may be extended (in Victoria) providing the party concerned can provide proof of sufficient funds to finance the extended stay.

Visitors are also asked to produce an onward or return flight ticket and confirmation of a hotel booking (minimum 3 days). Please note: it is not possible to enter the Seychelles with the intention of looking for a hotel once there: prebooking is mandatory.

Health Regulations
No vaccination requirements at the present time. Nor are visitors recommended to undertake any particular prophylactic measures.

Health Care
There is a well-equipped hospital in Victoria as well as smaller clinics in the various administrative districts of Mahé and on Praslin and La Digue. In case of an emergency – whether it be illness or an accident – treatment is available within the framework of the National Medical Service; fees vary according to treatment. Medicaments may be purchased in the pharmacy attached to the hospital or at either of the two dispensaries in Victoria. Adequate supplies of any drugs which are taken regularly or which may be needed in the course of your stay in the Seychelles should be brought with you from home.

Enquire in advance about what proportion of medical costs will be covered by any private health insurance scheme you may be a member of. In order to avoid additional expense, you'd be well advised to consider health insurance for the duration of your holiday. Any travel agent or insurance company will have details of "package" deals including accident, cancellation and baggage insurance.

Health Precautions
Particularly in the first few days after your arrival, don't underestimate the power of the sun, even if this is belied by a cooling breeze or overcast skies. Opt for a sun cream with a high protection factor; sunglasses and something for the head are also recommended. If snorkelling, guard against sunburn by wearing a T-shirt in the water.

Depending upon tides, sea urchins can be washed up on some beaches; sandals or similar afford protection for the feet. Should a spine of such a sea urchin become embedded in the foot, there's little point trying to remove it yourself. As with cuts and grazes from sharp coral, disinfect the wound thoroughly to avoid infection and a spoilt holiday. Otherwise the spine is best left alone; in time it will be absorbed by the body. There are a few "home remedies" which claim to speed up this process: some locals swear by vinegar poultices, others rub the affected area with lemon juice, others again apply hot wax. If in any doubt, consult a doctor.

You need have no reservations about eating fruit and raw vegetables. Water is also perfectly safe although it is recommended that you drink the water provided in jugs or carafes in hotel rooms.

Gnats and the like are not normally a problem (they are dealt with by monsoon winds and air conditioning in hotel rooms). If necessary, the hotel will supply an insect spray, which also helps to keep the number of flies down.

Should you find geckos on the ceiling or walls of your room, don't worry and don't try to chase them out; these small lizards are perfectly harmless and help to control the number of flies and other insects.

Language

Creole, which contains many elements of French, has been the national language since 1981. English and French are official languages, so communication should not prove problematic.

Flights to the Seychelles

Since the opening of the international airport in 1971, the aeroplane has taken over almost entirely from the boat as the sole means of access to the Seychelles. The shipping of freight remains a lively business and occasional cruisers deposit passengers on the islands, but otherwise flying in is the order of the day.

A number of airlines link the Seychelles with Europe, the Americas, Asia, Africa, Australasia and the other islands of the Indian Ocean.

At the present time (1990) both Air Seychelles and British Airways operate direct flights (both several times a week) between Great Britain and the Seychelles.

Air Seychelles also flies Singapore – Seychelles on a weekly basis, thus providing connecting flights for those coming from Australia, New Zealand, the Far East and Southeast Asia. Should you wish to fly from Great Britain to any of the above regions (or vice versa), you might like to take advantage of the exciting possibility of a stopover in the Seychelles.

For those travelling to the Seychelles from the United States and Canada, the easiest option is definitely via Europe. Doing so opens up a whole range of interesting flight connections, especially when seen in combination with the chance to see some of Europe en route.

Air France operates several flights weekly between North America and Paris, connecting there with direct flights to the Seychelles (Air Seychelles also has non-stop flights Paris – Seychelles).

In the same way, you could take in London by flying British Airways or any number of American airlines thus far and then continuing your journey with British Airways or Air Seychelles. Lufthansa, Alitalia and various American airlines fly to Frankfurt and Rome; Air Seychelles link both cities with the islands.

Combining your trip to the Seychelles with visits to other Indian Ocean islands (e.g. Réunion, Mauritius, Madagascar or the Comoro Islands) will mean little or no extra flight costs. Such an itinerary is best arranged with a travel agent, who will be able to advise as to the most advantageous deals on offer.

Another interesting combination might include beach holiday and safari in "neighbouring" East Africa; flight connections with Kenya Airways and Air Tanzania. Again, ask a travel agent for more details.

Flights within the Seychelles

Even as far as interisland transport is concerned, boats and ships have had to make way for the aeroplane. Air Seychelles operates two types of aircraft for those who are "island hopping": the 9-seater "Islander" and the newly acquired 20-seater "Twin Otter". There is a regular shuttle service between Mahé and Praslin; Frégate and Bird Island are linked with Mahé on a daily basis. There are flights to and from Denis Island and Desroches three times a week.

Car Hire

As a supplement to the chapter "Out and About in the Seychelles" (p.130), here now some facts and figures about car hire. Various types of car ranging from Minis to large Japanese models are offered for hire with free mileage. Charges per day (for a period of hire of 1-6 days) range between SR 250 and SR 370; for larger models you may pay up to SR 440 per day. When hiring for a period of 7-14 days, the rate per day will be between SR 200 and SR 330. Again, expect higher rates for larger models. International hire car firms are usually more expensive than local enterprises, so do shop around for good deals (often dependent upon the season). Car hire rates include tax; mileage is unlimited. When hiring, be sure to enquire about full insurance cover.

Fuel costs are extra and are very high. For example, in 1989, a litre of petrol cost SR 5.21 (i.e. approx. £ 0,60, US$ 0,95).

When you collect your vehicle, check how much petrol is in the tank; it's not unusual to find vehicles being handed over with tanks filled to only a quarter their capacity. In order to avoid being stranded somewhere without petrol, motorists should be aware that there are only five filling stations on Mahé. These are in Beau Vallon, in Victoria (Francis Rachel St.), opposite the airport, in Anse Royale and at the Seychelles Sheraton Hotel (in the latter case only between 7 a.m. and 3 p.m.). On Praslin you'll only find filling stations in Grand Anse and Baie Ste. Anne.

The driver of the hired car must be at least 21 years of age; there is no maximum age. A national driving licence suffices.

Most car hire firms can also provide cars with drivers. In this case you'll pay between SR 800 and SR 1500 per day.

Far and away the most popular vehicle is the Mini Moke, a jeeplike, open car. Rates per day are between SR 250 and SR 320, between SR 225 and SR 280 per day if hiring for a week (prices vary from company to company). Suzuki jeeps are now, however, beginning to challenge the Mini Mokes in the popularity stakes. Rates per day are between SR 250 and SR 350, and between SR 225 and SR 315 per day if hiring for a week. Here, too, you'll find there are considerable differences between high and low season rates.

Bicycle Hire

Bicycles are available for hire on Praslin and La Digue; you'll find prices are very high. The most reasonable rate per day (for a period of hire of several days) may in some instances be as much as SR 30-40.

Traffic Regulations

Traffic drives on the left. Speed limit within towns and villages is 40 km/h (25 m.p.h.), otherwise 65 km/h (40 m.p.h.).

Taxis

Taxis are not fitted with meters. Prices are fixed, however, for journeys between Victoria and the international airport and between the major hotels and places of interest on Mahé. Every taxi driver must carry a copy of the official tariff; the latter will also be available at hotel receptions. The best idea is probably to ask at the hotel beforehand what a particular journey will cost. The price you will be asked to pay may not correspond exactly with the official fare: some taxi drivers round off the final sum quite generously in their own favour, others don't. In the same way, it's left to the individual driver to decide whether and how much luggage is covered by the official surcharge of SR 5. To give some idea of the fares in question:
Airport to Reef Hotel SR 25;
Airport to Beau Vallon Hotels SR 70;
Airport to Barbarons Beach Hotel SR 80;
Victoria to Reef Hotel SR 60;
Victoria to Beau Vallon Bay Hotels SR 30.

Since it's often difficult to obtain a taxi in more remote areas (e.g. from restaurants in southwest Mahé) it's recommended that you make a definite arrangement with the taxi driver as to when he should return to collect you.

All the above prices refer to Mahé and are valid between 6 a.m. and 8 p.m. On Praslin prices are generally about 20 % higher. Between 8 p.m. and 6 p.m. a surcharge is levied on both islands.

The prices fixed for certain round trips by taxi are often just slightly higher than the cost of hiring a car (plus extra costs involved) for the same trip. In any case, be sure to agree on the price before setting out. The main taxi rank in Victoria is opposite the Anglican church, behind the main post office.

Bus Services

S.P.T.C. buses operate along practically all roads on Mahé, linking the capital Victoria with all towns, villages and hotels. Since buses represent the most important means of transport used by the Seychellois, they are extraordinarily cheap, fares ranging between SR 2 and SR 6 (i.e. averaging about $^1/_{10}$ of the taxi fare).

The main bus station in Victoria is in Palm Street opposite Unity House. There's more about the advantages and "techniques" of travelling by bus in the chapter "Out and About in the Seychelles" (see p.133).

Ferries and Shipping

Ferry lines cater in the first instance to the needs of the local population. Thus ferries cross from Praslin/La

Digue to Mahé in the mornings and make the return crossing in the afternoon, which means they can be used by tourists for trips with at least one overnight stay. For day trips from Mahé to other islands, make use of the services offered by local travel agents.

The ferries between Praslin and La Digue lend themselves well to half-day visits to La Digue, possibly combined with flights Mahé-Praslin-Mahé. You'll find package deals of this kind can be arranged at the travel agents' in Mahé.

The government ship "Cinq Juin", which supplies the Outer Islands, does in fact have accommodation for pleasure passengers. There are 12-day round trips to the Amirantes and 20-day trips to Farquhar/Aldabra. With the exception of Desroches (Amirantes group), none of the outer islands are equipped for tourist visits. Providing the "Cinq Juin" is not engaged outside Seychelles waters, departures are every two to three months (to the Amirantes and Farquhar/Aldabra in turn). Enquiries about departure dates and cruise prices are best made on the spot.

Chartering Boats
On Mahé, motor-boats can be hired for pleasure outings and deep-sea fishing from the Marine Charter Association in Victoria (P.O. Box 204, Port of Victoria, Tel.: 22126; the office is at the harbour, access via 5th June Avenue). Most hotels will also be able to arrange for a boat to be chartered; some in fact have their own charter service.

A half-day charter costs between SR 1,900 (boat for four persons) and SR 2,500 (six persons). For a whole day one should estimate SR 2,300-3,500. Charter prices include soft drinks, beer, fishing tackle and – in the case of a whole-day charter – a midday meal.

Boats for deep-sea fishing and snorkelling tours can also be hired on Denis Island.

Yachts and schooners with two to ten berths are available for charter (single day to several weeks) for excursions as far as Aldabra or for diving tours with the necessary equipment. Prices and conditions of hire from the Marine Charter Association in Victoria (address above) or from the Seychelles Underwater Centre (Beau Vallon; see addresses below); on La Digue, apply to La Digue Lodge. On certain day-long tours (for example, those organized by the Underwater Centre) it's possible to book single places at the cost of SR 600 per person. The same is true of diving tours lasting several weeks (to Aldabra, for example); the latter are not a regular feature.

Diving Schools and Bases
The following professionally operated and well equipped enterprises were in operation (late 1989/90):

**Big Game Watersports
(Thérèse Island)
Sheraton Hotel**
P.O. Box 540
Mahé
Tel: 78451

Fred Janker
**Blue Lagoon Watersports
Blue Lagoon Chalets**
P.O. Box 442
Mahé
Tel. 71197

Rick Howatson
**Marine Divers
Northolme Hotel**
P.O. Box 333
Mahé
Tel 47222

David Rowat/Glynis Sanders
**Seychelles Underwater Centre
Coral Strand Hotel**
P.O. Box 384
Mahé
Tel. 47357/47036

Bernard Camille
**Praslin Beach Hotel
Anse Volbert**
Praslin
Tel. 32222

Gregoire's Watersports
**La Digue Lodge
Anse la Réunion**
La Digue
Tel. 34233

Since the Seychelles lie outside the cyclone belt, diving can be enjoyed all year round (for more information, see "Sports in the Seychelles", p.141). In 1989 diving excursions by boat cost around SR 135 per dive; a "tenpack" for around SR 1,250. Night-time dives cost approximately SR 160, adventure diving (for example, to the wreck of the "Ennerdale"), some SR 240 per person (leaving from Beau Vallon).

Postal Charges, Telephone
Postcards by air mail and aero-grammes cost SR 2. First class airmail (10 g) SR 3, then SR 2 for every additional 10 g.

International direct dialling to Europe, approx. SR 30 per minute. Calling from a hotel incurs a surcharge (rates vary from establishment to establishment). It is possible to call direct from Cable and Wireless Ltd. in Francis Rachel Street, Victoria.

Business Hours
Banks: In Victoria, in general Mondays to Fridays 8.30 a.m. to 1 p.m. (in cases where banks do not reopen in the afternoon, they may well remain open until 2 or 3 p.m.). Branch offices – for example, in Beau Vallon – open from 9 a.m. to 12 noon. Some banks offer an afternoon and /or Saturday service: the Habib Bank and the Bank of Credit and Commerce International, for example, open on Monday to Friday afternoons between 2.30 p.m. and 4 or 4.30 p.m. The Bank of Credit and Commerce International,

together with the Banque Française Commerciale and Barclay's Bank International, also opens on Saturdays between 8.30/9 a.m. and 11.30 a.m./ 12.30 p.m.
On Praslin, banking hours (Barclay's) in Ste. Anne are Mondays to Fridays 8.30 a.m. to 12 noon; in Grand Anse, 2.30 p.m. to 3.30 p.m.

The bank counters at the airport open for the arrival and departure of all international flights.
Post Offices: Main post office in Victoria opens Mondays to Fridays 8 a.m. to 4 p.m., Saturdays 8 a.m. to 12 noon. In more remote regions it is possible to leave post at various police stations. Hotel receptions will, of course, accept and pass on their guest's post.

Air mail letters must reach the main post office by noon if they are to make the international departures that evening or the next morning.

Shops: Mondays to Fridays 8 a.m. to 5 p.m. (some close for lunch between 12 noon and 1 p.m.); Saturdays 8 a.m. to 12 noon. Main market day in Victoria is Saturday: business starts as of around 5.30 a.m. and continues well into the morning.

Electricity Supply
240 V AC. Most hotels have razor sockets for European appliances

Time Difference
Greenwich Mean Time + 4 (Central European Time + 3)

Service Charges and Tips
As a rule, a service charge is included in hotel and restaurant bills. In the case of smaller charges (for example in cafés), leave 2-3 rupees on the table if you were happy with the service; if the bill is higher, the tip should be 6-7 rupees.

Porters usually receive 1-2 rupees for each piece of luggage they carry, chambermaids 2-3 rupees per day of one's stay.

Otherwise, tipping is not normal practice, which is not to say that your taxi driver, for example, would not appreciate a few extra rupees.

Clothing
Light, airy beachwear and leisure wear – preferably in cotton – are usually all you'll need. Long-sleeved blouses or shirts are a useful addition as protection from the sun. Some kind of (lightweight) raincoat or an umbrella will come in handy should you encounter a heavy shower while out and about.

It is not done to wander about town in beachwear. Topless bathing on hotel beaches is tolerated though not encouraged; nudism is frowned upon in the Seychelles.

Customs Regulations
To the Seychelles: Personal items for everyday use may be imported duty-free. In addition, the following are not subject to duty: 200 cigarettes or 50 cigars or 250 g tobacco, 1 l. spirits, 1 l. wine, 125 cc perfume, 25 cl. toilet water and gifts worth up

to SR 400 (SR 200 for those under 18 years of age).

The importation of the following items is prohibited: arms (including air guns and air pistols), ammunition, spear guns, drugs. Neither may you bring the following goods with you to the Seychelles: seeds, plants, flowers, fruit, vegetables, tea, meat and meat products.

Out of the Seychelles: An export licence is required to take coco-de-mer nuts out of the country. This will be issued by any authorized dealer.

Holiday/Festivities Calendar

January 1/2	New Year
March/April	Good Friday, Easter
May 1	Labour Day
June 5	Liberation Day (parade)
June	Corpus Christi
June 29	Independence Day, National Youth Sports Festival
August 15	Assumption of Our Lady
September	La Fête La Digue, annual regatta
November 1	All Saints
November	Annual deep-sea fishing championship
December 8	Immaculate Conception
December 25	Christmas

Bibliography

The following works are available only on the islands
Seychelles, From One Island to Another, Claude Pavard;
Flowers and Trees of the Seychelles, Francis Friedmann (1986);
Coco de Mer, The Romance of a Palm, Guy Lionnet (1986),
Demeures d'Archipel Seychelles (a study of colonial architecture in the Seychelles; 1988).

The best selection of books in Victoria is to be found at NPCS Ltd., Huteau Lane (beside Barclay's Bank, on the corner of Albert St. and Huteau Lane). Many hotel boutiques will also stock one or more of these works.

Information

The headquarters of the Seychelles Tourist Office is in

Independence House (P.O. Box 92)
Independence Avenue
Victoria, Mahé
Tel: 22881
Fax: 21612

The Seychelles Tourist Office has branches in Great Britain and the United States.

Seychelles Tourist Office
2nd Floor, Eros House
111 Baker Street
London W1M 1FE
Tel: (01) 224-1670
Fax: (01) 487-5756

Seychelles Tourist Office
P.O. Box 33018
St. Petersburg, Florida 33733
Tel: (813) 864-3013
Fax: (813) 867-0796

Index

Contents

Please note:
Every effort was made to ensure that the information given was correct at the time of publication.

However, as it is not possible for any travel guide to keep abreast of all changes regarding passport formalities, rates of exchange, prices, etc., you are advised to contact the appropriate authorities (embassy, bank, tourist office…) when planning your holiday.

The publishers would be pleased to hear about any omissions or errors.

Hildebrand's Travel Guides

Vol. 1 Sri Lanka (Ceylon)
Professor Manfred Domrös and
Rosemarie Noack

Vol. 3 India, Nepal
Klaus Wolff

Vol. 4 Thailand, Burma
Dr. Dieter Rumpf

Vol. 5 Malaysia, Singapore
Kurt Goetz Huehn

Vol. 6 Indonesia
Kurt Goetz Huehn

Vol. 8 Hong Kong
Dieter Jacobs and
Franz-Josef Krücker

Vol. 9 Taiwan
Professor Peter Thiele

Vol. 10 Australia
Michael Schweizer and
Heinrich von Bristow

Vol. 11 Kenya
Reinhard Künkel and
Nana Claudia Nenzel
Contributions by
Dr. Arnd Wünschmann,
Dr. Angelika Tunis and
Wolfgang Freihen

Vol. 13 Jamaica
Tino Greif and Dieter Jacobs

**Vol. 14 Hispaniola (Haiti,
Dominican Republic)**
Tino Greif and Dr. Gerhard Beese
Contribution by Wolfgang Freihen

Vol. 15 Seychelles
Clausjürgen Eicke
Contributions by Christine Hede-
gaard and Wolfgang Debelius

Vol. 16 South Africa
Peter Gerisch and Clausjürgen Eicke
Contributions by Hella Tarara

Vol. 17 Mauritius
Clausjürgen Eicke
Contributions by Peter Gerisch,
Joachim Laux and Frank Siegfried

Vol. 18 China
Manfred Morgenstern

Vol. 19 Japan
Dr. Norbert Hormuth

Vol. 21 Mexico
Matthias von Debschitz and
Dr. Wolfgang Thieme
Contributions by Werner Schmidt,
Rudolf Wicker, Dr. Gerhard Beese,
Hans-Horst Skupy, Ortrun Egelkraut,
Dr. Elizabeth Siefer, Robert Valerio

Vol. 24 Korea
Dr. Dieter Rumpf and
Professor Peter Thiele

Vol. 25 New Zealand
Robert Sowman and
Johannes Schultz-Tesmar

Vol. 26 France
Uwe Anhäuser
Contribution by Wolfgang Freihen

Hildebrand's Guide de Voyage

Vol. 14 Hispaniola (Haïti,
République Dominicaine)

Vol. 15 Les Seychelles

Vol. 17 Ile Maurice, La Réunion

Hildebrand's Travel Maps
European Destinations

72. Austria 1 : 400,000
65. Belgium/Luxembourg 1 : 275,000
16. Cyprus 1 : 350,000
56. Czechoslovakia 1 : 700,000
66. Denmark 1 : 500,000
51. Europe 1 : 2,000,000
67. Finland 1 : 800,000
68. France 1 : 1,000,000
15. France/Corsica 1 : 200,000
69. Greece 1 : 1,000,000
13. Greece/Crete 1 : 200,000
50. Greece/Southern Mainland, Peloponnese 1 : 400,000
57. Hungary 1 : 600,000
70. Italy 1 : 1,000,000
7. Italy/Gulf of Naples 1 : 200,000,

Ischia 1 : 35,000
Capri 1 : 28,000
8. Italy/Sardinia 1 : 200,000
11. Yugoslavia/Yugoslavian Coast I North 1 : 400,000, General Map 1 : 2,000,000
39. Malta 1 : 38,000
20. Morocco 1 : 900,000
71. Netherlands 1 : 250,000
73. Poland 1 : 750,000
52. Portugal 1 : 400,000
6. Portugal/Algarve 1 : 100,000, Costa do Estoril 1 : 400,000
75. Spain, Portugal 1 : 1,000,000
1. Spain/Balearic Islands: Majorca 1 : 185,000, Minorca, Ibiza, Formentera 1 : 125,000

3. Spain/Canary Islands: Gran Canaria 1:100,000, Fuerteventura, Lanzarote 1 : 190,000
40. Spain/Majorca 1:125,000, Cabrera 1 : 75,000
4. Spain/Spanish Coast I Costa Brava – Costa Blanca 1 : 900,000, General Map 1 : 2,000,000
5. Spain/Spanish Coast II Costa del Sol – Costa de la Luz 1 : 900,000, General Map 1 : 2,000,000
2. Spain/Tenerife 1:100,000
74. Switzerland 1 : 400,000
19. Tunisia 1 : 900,000
41. Turkey 1 : 1,655,000
64. U.S.S.R/Western U.S.S.R. 1 : 3,500,000

Non-European Destinations

49. Africa/East Africa (Kenya, Tanzania) 1 : 2,700,000
32. Africa/South Africa 1 : 2,700,000*
31. Australia 1 : 5,315,000
54. Caribbean/French Antilles: Guadeloupe 1 : 165,000, Martinique 1 : 125,000
46. China 1 : 5,400,000
42. Cuba 1 : 1,100,000
18. Egypt 1 : 1,500,000
34. Hispaniola (Dominican Republic, Haiti) 1 : 816,000
28. Hong Kong 1 : 116,000, Macao 1 : 36,000
25. India 1 : 4,255,000
27. Indonesia/Western Indonesia 1 : 12,700,000, Sumatra 1 : 3,570,000,

Java 1 : 1,887,000, Bali 1 : 597,000, Sulawesi 1 : 3,226,000
17. Israel 1 : 360,000
23. Jamaica 1 : 350,000
45. Japan 1 : 1,600,000
44. Korea 1 : 800,000
38. Mauritius 1 : 125,000
43. Mexico 1 : 3,000,000
21. New Zealand 1:2,000,000
30. Philippines 1 : 2,860,000
53. Puerto Rico, Virgin Islands 1 : 290,000
55. Réunion 1 : 127,000
33. Seychelles General Map 1:6,000,000, Mahé 1 : 95,000, Praslin 1 : 65,000, La Digue 1 : 50,000, Silhouette 1 : 85,000, Frégate 1 : 25,000

26. Thailand, Burma, Malaysia 1 : 2,800,000, Singapore 1 : 139,000
59. United States, Southern Canada 1 : 3,500,000
United States/California 1 : 700,000
United States/Florida 1 : 700,000
United States/ The Northeast 1:700,000
48. United States/The East 1 : 3,500,000
United States/ Southern Rockies and Grand Canyon Country 1 : 700,000
47. United States/The West 1 : 3,500,000
76. The World

* in preparation

Notes

Notes

Notes

Notes

Notes

Notes

Notes